Loveship

By

Leon R. Walker Jr

Loveship is for *all races*. Learn approaches, techniques, and tools essential for your personal growth and relationship success.

For information, about speaking engagements and appearances, contact:

wleon4241@gmail.com

website: www.iinspireone.com

Instagram: Iinspireone

Facebook: Leon R. Walker Jr

Linkedin: Leon R. Walker Jr

Google: Leon R. Walker Jr

Youtube: Leon R. Walker Jr

ASIN:

Pring ISBN: 978-1-09834-096-4

eBook ISBN: 978-1-09834-097-1

Book and Cover Design by Dimitrinka Cvetoski; www.fiverr.com/dimidesign

Edited by David Connolly david.flameshot@gmail.com; www.fiverr.com/flameshot

First Edition: [Insert Month, 2020]

TABLE OF CONTENTS

Author's Note

I correspond to you, in Loveship, constructing a sequence of events based on how I and others have experienced relationships and the manner by which we perform in them, be it good, bad, or indifferent. When we *"fall"* in love, our hearts can sink, we may even let our guard down, and our head may fall. This can be misleading, for many. Collectively, our sights, love, pain, and hurt are neither foresight, nor hindsight when we desperately need them to be, to execute flawlessly. It is wishful thinking, but I lay out a plan to prepare you onward. Unfortunately, without the safeguard of many healthy relationship variables, we are at the mercy of toxins and viruses, yet still, Loveship renders an acute strategy for that as well. Women fall in love more than men do, when this occurs, *and it does very often*, becoming uncomfortable, uncertainty, and a clear lack of balance, supersedes many things—mainly the desire for true and genuine love and unity! On many occasions, an unfair existence will materialize, through singular, and one-sided dominance, for the man! As men, at least for me, my initial thought was always "man, I am crazy about her," or "Damn, I can't stop thinking about her." I think most men are ok with being crazy about someone as opposed to *"falling in Love!"* When we are crazy about you, it's usually concerning one or two things, and not you, as a whole. This becomes our safety net or defense mechanism. That leads us to have "precautions" for reasons, mostly unknown or if known, are tied to our childhood fears or insecurities, yet we deny these reasons. I wasn't saving myself for one woman, I was spreading myself for--all women! At any given moment of life, with reference to; passion, engaging in a relationship, or thinking about one, we naturally reserve an inclination for the best, and pray that we're safe in doing so. Those are key components. Although, in a perfect world, the direction of one's life path of solitude, eternal bliss, and functionality, are indubitably straight ahead, it's not in *Loveship*, and I penned it that way, on purpose. Because relationships, initially begin on a natural course, for the most part, but in due time, many things will transpire and for many reasons, wanted or unwanted, warranted or unwarranted. However, that being said, we still wish to entertain or ascertain a voracious, and wholesome relationship appetite, on account of our intellectual enchantment. This leads us to remain fair and steadfast in our efforts to understand those with inherent culpability. My book holds true as an honest testament, that is exceedingly, and thoroughly relatable. It has been derived from the depths of my heart and soul. You will learn and receive perspectives *fastened* with keen intuition that will no doubt, *emotionally disturb you*, yet perpetuate grace, growth, certainty, and a knack for the betterment of all and how to become a solid, unconditional, loving, man and woman. We hardly fall for women like they fall for us, and that must change.

Dedication

My book is dedicated to first, God, as he has put in my life, very loving and understanding people, namely, my parents Leon R. Walker "Zeke" Sr and my mother, Sylvia E. "Gypsy" Gaither. My brothers Donnie, and Ralph, and my very strong sister, Antoinette "Toni" Walker. As siblings, we argue, grow, and come closer together, and that we've done, regardless of the hands we were dealt. For that, I extend to you the military's highest honors--respect, admiration, and a sharp hand salute! There are a host of close friends that have given me advice, as well. I appreciate you for your acts of kindness and sage advice. To my children, Kayla, Kamarin, and Aamir, although we don't see eye to eye, and have had some misunderstandings in the past and present which come with life, please remember, Dad loves you unconditionally!

Acknowledgements

Aside from my parents, family, and close friends, I'd like to thank Master Chief Jonathan

Rivera, his wife, Quemeka Rivera, and their beautiful children. When I met you all in 2003 in Norfolk Virginia, I'd never imagined having someone in my life that prayed for me like you all have done and continue to do so. I had no clue how close we would become, nor did I ever imagine two Second Class Petty Officers being my mentors, keeping me straight and not judging me for my anger issues and egregious ways. I had a fear of letting you down, and that was my motivating factor to continue to do well, in the Navy and in life. I have always acknowledged you all, but more importantly, I want the world to know that you continue to save my life! You come highly regarded and esteemed as the married couple and family for many to emulate! I love you all with every inch of my being, my blood, soul, and my spirit--THANK YOU!

"YOU ARE NOT ONLY A MAN; YOU ARE A WO-MAN."

7LEON R. WALKER JR7

Aligned with the heavens and earth

1 CORINTHIANS 13:1

Love is patient, love is kind. It does not envy, it does not boast, it is proud. It is not rude, it is not self-seeking, it is not easily angered, it keeps no record of wrong. Love does not delight in evil but rejoices with the truth.

Don't Change...

Don't change, but rather exchange what you see in me.
For quite some time, you saw the things that I could not see.
I need your vision, even for the things I can't envision.
And when I struggle, help me make a decision.

Don't change, please, baby.
It might be strange, but finer things are not finer than you.
The most beautiful thing about us is that you keep me true.
Sometimes you care too much, but it gives me confidence,
knowing you'll be there when I need your touch.

Please, don't change.
Continue to care, to remain aware, just continue to be there.
And if I do change, it's not because of anything wrong.
You see, you made me strong, gave me an exchange for my weakness.
You gave me completeness, to seek this...uniqueness.

The finer things also, like listening to you.
I see you, and your physique is just...immaculate.
You're what I want, luscious and succulent – you enter my soul.
You're heaven sent, remain as you are, I'm coming back to you.
I know it took some time, and even sounds strange,
but the time away was for me to get myself together.
So baby, please don't change!

"LISTENING – OR ITS LACK THEREOF – IS AN ART. I HEAR YOU WHEN I'M NOT INTO YOU, BUT WHEN I AM INTO YOU, I LISTEN SO THAT I CAN PROCESS IT ALL. THIS IS WHEN THE RELATIONSHIP EITHER STARTS OR ENDS."

~LEON R. WALKER~

Introduction

LOVESHIP is the testimony of my checkered past, as well as a lifestyle and relationship guide that is closely based—*word for word, experience for experience, with complete honesty*—on my **thirty-seven** years of relationship experience in and out of the United States Navy, period.

As you read further, you'll discover, devour, imprint, absorb, deeply sense and digest my views, experiences and vision, which will undoubtedly offer you a profound and firsthand look at certain types of character traits that can be found in a man, especially such as myself—traits that I either inherited, harbored, lived with, became engulfed in, or settled into. All the stories, analogies, behavioral inclinations, thought processes, and indulgences exhibited in this book are 100% true, and accurate, drawn from my lifetime of relationships. We're talking *thirty-seven weak and strong years* here. I have had a plethora of heartache, pain, learning, unlearning, and God-inspired awakenings. I have lived in, and through them all.

I do not believe much in hoping or wishing, because when you rely solely on hope and wishful thinking, you put the onus on someone else—and by placing the responsibility for an outcome on someone/something else, you send a clear and precise message to yourself and others that you are still seeking *outside* of one's self. It is not only counterproductive, but also gives you a false sense of improvement while in the true sense, you are under *imprisonment!* This will not only cause you to remain stuck in a state of suspended animation, but also render you susceptible to becoming easily fooled, misled, 'woman-handled' and manhandled! This is the basic notion.

In some other cases, people choose the cowardly path of "misery loves company". Those who choose this route to healing will never realize full and lasting healing because of their tendency to seek echo-chamber opinions that only reinforce their preconceived ideas. They would only inform people who will tell them exactly what they *want* to hear and not what they

✱ *need* to hear. If you seek out like-minded people, you are not looking for change; you're just looking for an *exchange*! ✱

While seeking help from a trusted source – perhaps from a very mature man or woman – for your own discernment and inner dealings is delightful, and does work, *your pivot-point* is still yours, not theirs! They *can be* an integral part, however.

Will it be hard to make the change? Yes, but what would be harder, at this point, is having to live with the regret years later about "what could have been" as opposed to what currently is.

I believed in my demons, and have exercised them unfairly to my advantage in the past, but now, I live in and exercise my God-given blessings to home in on a true and downright self-satisfying soul search. One that has *stripped* me down and turned me out from the inside out, but has cleansed my soul nonetheless—a much-needed cleansing.

I am ashamed, thoroughly embarrassed, but most of all, proud to be able to show you my growth and development, first from becoming intricately aware of and studying my mother, years after her death, while residing *"Inside the Box."*

I am equally qualified – by way of experience – to give you my play-by-play and accurate diagnosis of the many facets of dealing with relationships. How so? Well, I *was* the man that got it completely wrong on every level. It's rather easy to talk about what's right and the "feel-good's" in a relationship. However, not too often do we truly bare our souls regarding ✱ not just our inadequacies, failures, and our ability to do right or be honest, but also our failure or refusal to be open, honest, and ask for help.

I am giving you crystal clear examples and parallels that are not only derived from my brokenness, but are actual things you need to know, look out for, expect, build towards, and become aware of. This by no means *a tell-all,* and neither am I pointing fingers at anyone. I simply want to help women avoid meeting men like my past self, and to help men to cease encountering or desiring women that are just as broken, afraid, or dysfunctional as they are. In the event that they do meet these dysfunctional individuals, my goal is that they'll be very well prepared and equipped to deal with him/her, or not—either way, you'll know.

Additionally, for the men, this book is to help you avoid befriending men like my past self, and to hold up a mirror to help you see myself in you, regardless of your age. In doing so, I will make you comfortable in your transition to transparency by "Presenting Your Past" during any dialogue you wish, in order to lead you to the woman of your dreams, but first, you have to discover yourself! I am not Pro-Man. It's obvious that I am a man; however, I only pride myself now on being able to Pro-Duce! Women want results that are not only written in stone, but also, don't end up on a tombstone! For some, this is just paying lip service.

Military men suffer a lot, just like other men, but on some occasions, we suffer much more, which ultimately hinders or destroys our ability to process many things. For me, they were honesty, love, affection, and in some cases, understanding. This book is for men and women alike. Some men might not want to read this, and I understand. Just remember, please, that some of you are who I once was. All of my addictions, egregious ways, and transgressions had *many* faces! With my evolution and transformation however, they no longer wore my face, and you can change yours too. Don't be afraid to do so, just try to read a little each moment, and you may find that maybe, just maybe, you *can* relate.

Some of my issues stemmed from my PTSD from numerous deployments to hostile enemy territories. However, most of our issues in general – if not all – *derive* from our childhoods. At least that was the case for me.

"ONCE YOU BECOME UNAFRAID TO CONTACT AND CONSULT YOUR PAST LIKE YOU CONTACT AND CONSULT PHYSICIANS, THAT'S WHEN YOUR CHANGE STARTS. GET UP, WAKE UP, AND MAKE AN APPOINTMENT WITH YOUR PAST. DON'T BE LATE, AND DON'T CANCEL!"

~ LEON R. WALKER JR~

I was given the perfect playing field by the devil to be deceitful, cunning, luring, rude, discourteous, impolite, uncivil, and ill-mannered, amongst many more despicable qualities. However, because of that, I was able to understand women much better, either from experiencing rejection, having my foolery and trickery exposed, or just being called out on my BS! I have now become extremely intuitive with regard to a woman's DNA— especially my mother's!

The best way to know, understand, and love a woman, is to start with understanding your own mother and your relationship to her. Your woman and mother are two different people, yet, in many ways, they share the same roles. By taking a deep dive into my mother's life, her ways, fears, thought processes, and strengths, I became uniquely equipped to understand women from a different perspective. For her teachings, in life and in death, and for the invaluable lessons I learned, I now appreciate my mother for passing down those wonderful gifts.

I salute you, Mommy!

My mother was short and thickset, but she stood up to much bigger and stronger men when she needed to. That, in itself, taught me that no matter how you looked at a woman, they still held an immense power: the power to make you better if you heed their teachings, or show that you'll eventually become worse if you don't! From this, I also learned that most men often look to other men for guidance concerning their women, which is one of the worst mistakes a man can make, unless the man whose counsel is being sought tells him the God-given truth, from *his* loss! Sometimes, what you tell another fella can be held against you, so be careful with that.

Broken men break women down to their own level of life, hurt, pain, discomfort, and dysfunction. That level becomes his comfort zone, and hers too, because she'll love him unconditionally, thus losing herself! Losing herself is an act of desire that stems from her empty void of hurt, lack of

love, and attention, one which she's expecting to be filled. This void, how- ✳
ever, will not be filled by a broken man— it can only be drained further!

Please do not be alarmed. As a former military man, my actions, perfor-
mance, progress, and healing milestones were reached and accomplished
through help, growth, and many months of therapy. I am not a "Throwaway
Guy" by any means. I went to and through the depths of hell, but I returned
a much better person and partner for a woman. You'll figure that out from
the conversations that we are about to have as I discuss the greatness,
strengths, and on some occasions, the weakness of both partners, in thor-
ough detail.

Again, the narratives here are not only applicable to military men. I was a
young man before I entered the Navy. The Navy exposed me to beautiful
people, strong men and women, and the best services that allowed me to
stay alive. Yet in doing what I did, and living the way I lived, my choices
clearly weren't indicative of someone wise enough to take advantage of
the extended services and quality people I had access to or was exposed
to. I was weak within and during my toxic endeavors!

Throughout my thirty-seven years of dating, break-ups, make-ups, and
marriage, I have studied, and found the most intricate, intimate, intuitive,
and engaging nouns that suit any relationship universally:

Friendship, Courtship, Companionship, and Leadership.

Through the hurt and pain, you must remain focused on these; they mature
and develop as you progress on your search and journey, but only with the
right person—your teammate!

T.E.A.M. = Teach, Endure, Assess, Marry!   ✳

Before implementing any of these in a relationship, you must know the
✳ person you're with and vice-versa. They must be willing to pass certain
checkpoints in your relationship—this is crucial! Before everything starts

to run smoothly in your life, there will unavoidably be some dysfunction, flaws, setbacks, and heartache. I discuss these throughout the book.

My testament is for little boys, girls, young men, and young women alike, because that's where it all began for me, and it never left. As an adult, I surely needed these chapters and discussions— but let's start with my childhood. First, let's all take a step back to reminisce, contemplate, and introspect, that is if you want to improve yourself as a man or woman in a relationship. If not, then don't look back. I will warn you, though. Not looking back to those mentally torturing days, moments of fear, times of weakness, bad times, dysfunction, and anything else that you are running from will lead to them creeping up on your blind side when you are least expecting it. So, always look back to face and resolve your past to see the face that it wears, because those times do have a distinct face. ✳

As a true and defining guide in **Loveship,** I use and infuse one of the *best, strongest,* and *most compelling* leadership skills that have served me well to transcend myself – and you, potentially – to the next level of giving, understanding, teaching, sharing, receiving, visualizing and mentoring. I did not wait for my Sailors to ask me for advice, ever. Therefore, I will not make you wait, either. My Sailors, students, and other individuals that I continue to mentor get the real deal from me, and you will, too. I called my transformation *"Presenting My Past,"* and as hard as it was, I learned to do it.

In presenting my past, the future vision of our TEAM—(YOU AND I)— will become clear and exact concerning many things. For one, your courage will soar, in that you will now possess the ability to be honest with first yourself, and then your companion. You will become more forgiving and let go of any ill feelings, simply by presenting your past to someone as a future partner. Their trust will grow with you, but more importantly, a woman will be more engaged and eager to grow, overall, with you.

First, you must want self-preservation. In the act of preserving yourself, you pause all future negativity—the "pause" is your time to reflect, realize, accept, and redefine *YOU*. It's never too late. By speaking to you about my transition, I am giving you a true account of life-changing and life-altering events that reshaped how I looked at, learned, treated, and then understood myself, by understanding the great women that were once in my life. I had to become keenly aware of their wants, needs, desires, and something else that many men overlook—their aspirations.

I was someone that always felt like women always wanted to control me. Therefore, I was always guarded with the women in my life. What I didn't know or realize at the time was that the woman usually discovered my immaturity and inability to walk with her while she was trying all along to walk with, or catch up to me, who was intent on running away. She just wanted more out of life with me, so she felt compelled to hold me accountable and "control" me—which turned out to be nothing more than guidance—so that we could build an "account" together. By "account," I am not talking about money here, but how often do men realize that they are either "IN A RELATIONSHIP" or "INVESTING IN A RELATIONSHIP?" Women hate to waste time, but as men, we could care less about time and thus miss out on invaluable *INVESTMENTS* we can make in that *ACCOUNT!* She was only trying to make me better.

Accountable = Able to be accounted for, being present, aware, relied upon, not absent!

Being intricately involved with your woman, without fear of being led by her, her aspirations will become your inspiration! This is why I convey my stories and experiences the way that I do **in *Loveship.***

The transition will be accomplished without any hesitation or embarrassment that will follow from "relating" to my stories. As I *presented my past*, I began to see certain transgressions or bad habits in other people before they saw it in themselves. This is a gift that I have, and I am going to share all of my gifts, and pain, in an effort to make you see, attain and become familiar with your gift for yourself. In life, we too often wait until it's too late. *Loveship* will definitely prevent you from waiting too late ever again!

No, I am not a love doctor, and neither am I a relationship guru, yet I have amassed many emotional wounds and only closed them through months of therapy. The ones that remain open are for the light of God to heal—those ✳ wounds are reserved for Him, as there isn't any social worker, psychologist, or psychiatrist, in my opinion, that can close them. No disrespect to any of those professionals that tried, but my stigmata belonged to God, and *that* was beyond their reach!

These concepts of friendship, courtship, companionship, and leadership – in no particular order of priority – are *must-haves* in order to perceive, believe, achieve with, and not to deceive *anyone*! These traits will undeniably grant you the ability to identify, *directly or indirectly,* with your understanding of people and their lives, before reacting from an emotional standpoint and a broken or disappointed state of mind. Broken people do not possess these traits. While some might, it'll always be partial, based on their wants, needs, greed, fear, or lack of a clear vision to grow, all due to a malfunctioning moral compass!

Throughout the years, I have suffered, cried, begged, pleaded, and even ✳ stalked. I have also hurt plenty of women—women who unfortunately found themselves on my destructive path, or the ones that I deceived enough into liking, loving, and hating me and my dark, dirty, self-centered, egotistical, narcissistic, psychopathic world. Some women are just as bad as men. They understand you better, just like you, and can relate. All the other women and I had become unique parts of each other's broken mirrors. We put our pieces back together. However, the jagged brokenness remained obvious. We became mirrored images, and during our mending, the only thing we shared was our shattered exterior!

None of us got help!

To the reader, no matter your race, color, creed, or gender, the journey that I am about to take you on will surely open your eyes to your current and future situation. In life, many people hurt, become confused, are used, abused, taken advantage of, left behind, looked over, forgotten about, and neglected. I give to you—from my heart—my pain, successes, and failures, and how to recover, heal, and grow! I lay out early signs of deceit and dysfunction, from my perspective and *men*-tality. I give you a clear and concise vision—a vision that you may never have thought about until now. I give you a heartfelt, open, and honest viewpoint, and *NO ONE* is excluded—gay, transgender, it doesn't matter. You all have been *INCLUDED*. Most people like to and want to *EXCLUDE* you, but I will not, *ever*! You are just as human, but mainly, even more courageous than many! Some of you have had to hide your identity, life, and lifestyle, but you shouldn't—and it's time to stop!

Before we go any further, I want you to come to know *me* first, as a prelude to our further discussions, so that you can receive, digest, and understand the *full-fledged* synopsis of who I was and why I became that person. There are millions of little boys, young and grown men, just like me. This portion of my story is just as crucial as the rest of the entire book.

Prologue

As a seven-year-old kid, I watched thousands of hours of porn. After my mind and body became used to it, the next step was to home in on how the women in those adult movies were reacting to touch, direction, arousal, kisses, sweat, tears of joy, aggression, pleasure, and obedience. I studied the women in porn to hurt women outside of porn, not to love them. They hurt me first—this was what I thought. I felt a surge of power engulf my entire being from my learning. It became a form of protection. *You'll never hurt me again!* Love lost!

I wanted to take over their minds, their souls. I planned to manipulate their blood flow, in order to shift the function of their circuitry in every part of their body. By mastering that, I managed their heartbeats and mindsets.

I was raped and molested by three women. Because of this, I allowed the devil to use me to portray him. It had become my duty to pay it forward. The man who touched me too…well…that trajectory steered me onto a course of plotting to harm pedophiles. I never did; that's not saying that I didn't get the chance to, but my anger issues were more directed against the theft of my innocence and virginity. As a molested, abused, bullied, and raped little boy, my Friendship, Courtship, Companionship, and Leadership path was derailed too soon after birth. I was only eight when I lost my virginity! My little mind was still developing.

Chapter One

A Couple Hundred

INTERACT-INTERCHANGE-INTERCOURSE-INTERCEDE-
INTERJECT

The five "I's" will help you and your partner discover your INNERMOST!
A *COUPLE HUNDRED* is deeply felt!

The concept of a fifty-fifty investment by partners is by far the most over-
rated idea of what to give, and how much to commit, in a relationship. By
proceeding into any relationship with the notion of "fifty-fifty" being fair,
you are already at a loss! Grade yourself and you will see where there's
a clear level of attrition! As we all know, there are many variables in a
relationship. We've been told that a 50/50 split is fair. Now, think back
to elementary school. Back then, we were taught that fifty percent is an
"F minus" grade! Therefore, the rudimentary concept of 50/50 alone, is
not fair. It's easily off by a clear fifty percent for both. For those of you
who believe giving fifty percent is fair, you are sadly mistaken. In some
cases, you may even have some selfish ways. Think more on the level of
100/100, encompassing 200 percent, and I'll explain.

As I speak about "Love Languages," I myself, am a total giver, but that's
not why I agree with the idea of "fifty-fifty" being inaccurate and mislead-
ing. Here is why. We'll assume that listed below are the areas in which you
plan to give fifty percent.

Spiritual support
Financial support
Physical support
Mental support

Moral support

As you see, I indiscriminately chose five categories, and these are great categories but by no means all-inclusive. So, if you're dead set following your fifty percent rule, then, you can only give each one of these categories ten percent of your attention! A relationship doesn't have a chance of survival with so little giving in each area. Please remember that there are many more categories to choose from. You can choose any trait that you plan to expend your fifty percent effort on, but regardless of how you look at it, and how good you feel about it, your effort and grade still amounts only to an "F minus!" Of those five categories that I chose above, I didn't exercise care or effort in all five areas. So during my relationships, I went into them as a depleted and incensed man. If you believe in the fifty-fifty rule, you will too! On average, I was operating at probably thirty percent in all my relationships, leaving my woman to struggle for the remaining 170 percent. Looking back on it, I regret the daunting tasks I left those women. In addition, it was also a clear indicator of my short-comings and inability to perform well in a relationship. My relationships were not able to survive. Instituting and living by my thirty percent mindset back then became the infamous destroyer of all women I dated, so please, make your hindsight--your foresight. You can implement foresight, by reflecting on past relationships or your old ways, and perform well in new relationships. This concept is called *"From End to Beginning;"* it's a real-life, deep mental imagery process. A reverse thought process that, *as I state in my chapter about cheating,* will propel you to think before you react to your feelings of seeking attention outside of your relationship. It will also grant you the ability to perceive how much pain and struggle you have left or are leaving your partner to handle. By taking the time to exercise *"From End to Beginning,"* you'll learn the potential of increased danger of what you're doing wrong, what you have done wrong or what you're not doing well. It will forecast your sights in an effort to calculate, gauge, and prevent future casualties and missteps. You will then find a truer, more in-depth, appreciation for your partner and what you have taken for granted!

Earlier I mentioned 200 percent since I truly believe that as partners, we should each give 100 percent to a relationship. Here is why. If for some reason I lose twenty, thirty, or forty percent, as a couple, we're still well above the 100 percent level and operating like a well-oiled machine. The same goes for your partner. If he or she loses any part of their 100 percent, you support them until they can give 100% again. When you meet a man like I was, one that's okay with you cooking, cleaning, and taking care of them in bed, he's only a "thirty-percenter." He will not expect anything else from you, nor will he give you anything else. In return, he'll match your thirty percent with what he is giving you. Equally, the two of you are now operating at sixty percent, a mental annotation of a "D" grade! Your efforts were only exhausting your energies because you were giving based upon someone else not being a fulfiller and yourself forgetting to operate in your true Love language of "Acts of Service!" Your misery is obvious because you are not being *you*! I mention this later in my book when we discuss Relationship *Mismatch.*

"Shiiiit, baby, I cook and clean, too—and you know, I blew your back out last night."

When a man blurts out these words, he truly feels like he's doing his part—he is, at least the thirty percent that you've accepted for many years! Conversely, there are some women who only give their "measly" thirty percent. A lot of women feel since they look good, put him to sleep after sex, and cook a great meal, they're good to go! No! Men have more needs, desires, and wants, just like women. Many men want to be heard, appreciated, and well respected. We are providers in many ways. Yes, some may not provide based on what you think we should provide, but, like I mention in *Loveship,"Your delivery is very important"* in how you convey your wants, needs, and desires, to him. Men don't require much, so do not take advantage of that.

As a retired Naval Veteran, there are two very significant roles that I must discuss along with the fifty-fifty. *The Homemaker and Ombudsman* roles. As I served thirty-two years in the Navy, every command employs an OMBUDSMAN. OMBUDSMAN means "Keeper of The People. Men and women service personnel both perform this role. They know the danger of the fifty-fifty rule all too well and anything less than giving 100 percent can be devastating to personnel onboard ships and at training commands. Most of them have experienced it quite often yet they continue to keep their heads up, shoulders back, and march forward, with pride and dignity. Both are well respected because they turn houses into homes and are an integral part of a well functioning military command! OMBUDSMAN are often sought out for sage advice, parental guidance, and marital wisdom, they too, carry a heavy burden. Now, Homemakers carry a heavy burden of many people and expectations, as well, while infusing the highest level of nurturing, *bar none*! Homemakers are not only leaders, but they're deep thinkers, too. Homemakers have a clear mindset of the home and everything that comes with running a household. They can be quite busy. Homeschooling, emotional balancing, and leadership, are just a few activities that homemakers are responsible for and employed to do. Contrary to popular belief, homemakers are very creative, in that they possess an innate ability to make use of time and master quality time. They are great managers, very well balanced, resourceful, and can expand utilization. They are also focused visionaries so be mindful of their gift and hard work! Homemakers are on the frontline serving and protecting. They deserve all of the accolades, coupled with the admiration!

As a Homemaker, some families are ok with the husband or wife serving in that capacity; it all depends on the agreement between the partners while dating or discussing marriage. Both parties must be clear in your intentions. A lot of partners will not necessarily speak up when asked by the other about being a "stay-at-home parent." Some partners might not want to agree to it because it places all of the financial responsibilities on one person. I can understand not wanting anyone else raising your kids, and there are some disabilities that prevent some from working in certain capacities, very understandable. Unfortunately, some men and women have done this for so long that it has now become completely alien and against their values to work outside of the home. I applaud men and women that stay home and raise the kids, but you can't become too comfortable with that because you definitely have more in you. Take some time to be *Known in the world of the Unknown* to keep your mind sharp and to also besiege yourself and family with new and exciting ideas. If you can't work outside of the home, consider a job where you can make money at home, even if it's just a couple hundred dollars per week. That extra money can be used to pay down bills, gas money, desired cups of rejuvenating coffee, a snack, haircut, a well earned visit to the spa or even a nice surprise for your partner. You can go to school online to further your education or learn a new skill. You can even create and sell items online or start an "at home" podcast!

By continually working together in a 100/100 partnership, your relationship becomes stronger. For example, paying the bills as a couple, you are both aware of how much money is being used each month. Debt can put a large strain on a relationship. A conversation about money becomes much easier when you are both aware of how much is being spent. Every once ✳ in a while, take time to reassess what your percentage of giving is in each area! Raising the kids, paying the bills, preparing the meals, sex—keep in mind, the kids get older, bills may be reduced and paid off, and you just might become a "twenty-percenter." It can happen slowly over time and some don't even realize they have reached that level!

Remember, the husband or wife that early on agreed to you staying home, will on occasion, lose themselves too. It is important to keep each other upbeat, by infusing reassuring confidence. You must also be in tune with their mindset, current mood, or even mood swings. Becoming very complacent and comfortable will have a tendency to set it, and this may not be either person's fault, but could be a clear indicator of one possibly losing interest! You must query and continue to address the relationship or marriage vows. As I also state in my chapter about revisiting *Relationship Vows*, this will assist with many things. It will help keep each partner on their toes, and continue to cultivate the seeds of love, affection, unity, growth, and why you all grew in love in the beginning.

For all those that remain or settle in a relationship, the longer you stay with your partner in their thirty percent, the more you'll continue to lose yourself and wonder why you don't feel complete. You're not in a relationship, and neither are you in a marriage – you're in a 50/50 raffle. Sometimes, you get nothing in return for what you've put into those raffle buckets! If you're lucky, you may get fifty percent back but that will not be enough over time. There are people who agree with the 50/50 rule because they may be already halfway out of the relationship! One painful but key thing to remember is: don't ever think that your partner is always happy; some divorces are surprises!

Chapter Two

Energy Light Zones

Becoming intricately involved with the energy of your partner is pivotal! This is knowledge that you must gain. Energy levels are precious; it's an equal understanding of who they are, what they like, love, enjoy, and are interested in. Energy is light, and light is power. When your partner is in their Energy Light Zone, this is your time to be supportive, thoughtful, and engaging. Balancing will begin to develop. You must act on it, take it in, manage it, and include this in your daily routine, not just when they're at the apex of their energy zone. Energy zones occur when their interest and passion meet. This can happen at any time throughout the day or a lifetime. The powerful encounter may happen during a conversation or while enjoying something they love, ie: camping, making candles, feeding animals, talking, knitting, dancing, wedding planning, working on a car, painting, singing, reading, cooking, thinking, making music, baking, playing an instrument, decorating a home, or building a business. Do not shut them out when they are in their Energy Zone; they're creating through their gift! You must support them, regardless if it is something you are interested in or not. Confidence and self-esteem are flourishing for your partner during this time. It is a time to form a deep, profound bond and create mutual respect for one another.

Once you understand this, relationship circuitry flows consistently and smoothly in the Energy Light Zone. Securing current and future success and growth during your partners' Energy Zone times while building ongoing continuity, you are also instilling empowerment, partnership reliance, stronger faith, dependence, and garnered trust. To take their Energy Zone to unprecedented levels, you must include appropriate touching—intermittent hugs, short kisses, and shoulder rubs. This demonstrates your commitment to their success. If your spouse is home performing in their Energy

Zone for friends or family, a short text containing words of encouragement seals the deal! It is imperative to encourage your children to support your partners' Energy Zone as well. This helps a child to learn about their own Energy Zones, too.

Chapter Three

Her Body

What I saw in porn, I wanted. The looks, lip size, shaved or hairy vulvas, positions, sounds, you name it. I wanted it all. It all became a part of my broken foundation. I was dead set on a certain breast size, a certain lipstick color, lip gloss, short hair, long hair, the kind that you could pull. The more I mastered certain body parts, the more I wanted! Each body part had a certain feeling that most people don't even know about. I became used to the porn and the sex itself began to bore me. I made sure to note the women's facial expressions. I even knew when they were faking.

These body portions (I call them portions because you will have an appetite for her while pleasing her) are listed at the end of my book and are not for anyone under the age of twenty-five, respectfully. These are treats for you and your man! They are not in any particular order. In fact, as you pay more attention to your woman, you'll learn what she likes, wants, and needs. However, the more sensual, nice, and pleasant you are to her, either during the day, week, or around other people, the faster she'll warm up. Respect, attention, eye contact, and being attentive to her, means a lot. Close to the end of this book, I will explain each body portion at a time.

PEARLS

- If you cheat and think that taking a shower before you get home, works, it doesn't. The scent of another woman comes from the inside, and not the outside. Your partner can easily smell this because your body scent has changed. She'll take note of this for weeks, or maybe even months and the signs will build and build and build. Your partner will not say anything, for the most part, until they have enough proof. You'll continue cheating because she's quiet, and as you continue, you dig a deeper hole. After your lies continue, when she knows all too well what you're doing, this is when her exit plan begins. Her questions were your chances to come clean.

- Don't ever be afraid to tell a strong woman, the truth. She's strong because the lies she's dealt with have made her strong, which made her an even deeper thinker, and more aware.

- If a person tells you "You're too deep," this means that they're ok with being shallow, move on! ✳

- Once the sex isn't good, it means that someone has checked out. This is when "one way" emotions begin. Aside from it being toxic, it now becomes a virus and runs on a course, concurrent to the entire relationship. Things will faltar and the two of you will be "off-kilter".

- Whenever she has mood swings, swing them back, with *good things!*

- If you cry after being rejected for sex, make sure you determine if it's becasue you're horny or feel unloved. Those are two very different emotions. Both will hurt your pride and ego, but one will make you get your toy and the other will make you hit him with a toy. There's another difference in crying yourself to sleep and going to sleep because you've climaxed! Knowing the difference, will help you to reexamine your sex life.

- Find out which dimension she's in, and then get into it. It'll help your vision, wisdom, and your ability to understand and know her, more.

- Men leave women that hold us accountable, for me, I then went to the ones that didn't have any "accounting data". ✳

- Renew your wedding vows often. The rules, regulations, and laws don't matter. Do it whenever you want to, and make it a surprise

- You say that you won't date a man who pays child support, yet you want to receive adult support. Be proud of a man that puts you second only to his kids. ✳

✳ • A beautiful personality is better than a pretty face. ✳

Chapter Four

Get Past Your Past

Following my abuse, I became closed-minded and cold-hearted over the course of time, unable to get past my past. I desperately needed to. However, my past, for many years, remained my present. ⭐

Ladies, you need to know a man and many more things about him if you desire to have a healthy, truthful, honest, fair, and forgiving relationship ⭐ with him. This also applies to your son. For instance, how many of you have asked your man, woman, or child about their past. I mean, their deep, dark past? Have you considered openly discussing their flaws, weak- ⭐ nesses? If not, you'll experience them, firsthand, in a very bad way. You'll become their first line of *offense*. At that time, there won't be much you can do about it except for taking in the abuse, be it financial, sexual, men- ⭐ tal, physical, or spiritual, simply because neither of you prepared for it— but you can prepare. Some remain too long in hopes of a flowery future. ⭐ When you do however, you might get the flowers you always wanted, but they'll be next to your casket! ⭐

If you don't delve into your partner's past, you are at the beginning stages of preparing for an assault, offense, or abuse of any kind. If you do speak about their past during the meeting of the minds, hearts, souls, and spirit (all four have to be present), you are now in a position to help each other. Please keep in mind that this doesn't mean you will spend the rest of your life with him or her, neither does it mean that you have found your soulmate. What it does mean, though, is that you are now finding yourself, and what you really want or are about to get—which is the most important person, in *yourself* not them!

You have a choice in the "Red Flag" avoidance or encounter, making the war of attrition more likely to be shorter, early on, or postponing the inevitable. In addition, "Red Flags" will become acutely clear, much earlier on in a relationship or in life.

Let me draw a parallel here. For instance, let's talk about the foundation of a house as an investment for a brief moment. Let's say you either have a great credit score, cash, or both. You've located a lender, one that's willing to work with you because they've looked to see if you qualify already, and you have checked them out in the Better Business Bureau too, with both of you asking the right questions (past, and present history). Everyone is happy, for the moment. Now to the construction: the foundation is laid – a solid ground, a thick, impenetrable sheet of mixed cement. It's the base or *basis* for future growth, development, additions, strength, and support. It's the root, put down firmly, with expected longevity and staying power!

I had that foundation; most people do. However, if laying that slate isn't done correctly, the foundation will crack, lean, leak, and then crumble! People put more preparation, time, energy, and effort into buying a home but come to discover later that it's really just a house and not a home. Some start to build just to show status—for attraction, to lure, and in some cases, fill a void, maybe even a lifelong dream. They wanted a house, not a home. The same parallel can be drawn with my relationships with women. We had the mutual intent to build, but it slowly faded. I was the house buyer without any future intent to stay around. It's much easier to leave a house, and so I suppressed my abandonment issues. I wanted women—not a woman!

My mother was a great woman and my father was a great man. They're now both deceased, yet I learn more from them now than I did in their lifetimes. Not because they did anything wrong—they raised me well—but because, relationship-wise, I didn't do much right. We're talking morals here. After studying my dad in death – a man of character whom I held in high esteem – I came to realize that he wasn't a womanizer. He was monogamous, but I became a womanizer. *I* chose that path. I neither listened to nor heeded to my mother's warnings, even though she was a great listener and deep thinker. I was simply not thoughtful at all.

We all have choices, of course, but we're often not taught early enough what I am about to teach you. Very few kids are taught this. I resonated more with my perpetrators and their evil intent and not my parents' teachings, both directly and indirectly. In the subsequent chapters are contained not just warnings, but lessons, aids, testimonials, and analogies. You're going to get it all, good and bad, happy, and sad! Be prepared to gain your *savoir-faire!*

Chapter Five

Their Past

Lesson One: Ask.

Many social experts are of the opinion that you should not ask questions about someone's past in early interactions. I disagree, *totally and whole-heartedly.* YOU'D BETTER, and here's why.

Asking about a potential partner's past can be frightening, but it can also be liberating and safe! Had the women in my life asked about my past as a child during conversation, they could have done or learned many things! At the point of asking, interrogating, or interviewing, whichever you choose, her safety – in a warm and comforting way – becomes strict and clear hindsight, during the *present* conversation. Hindsight doesn't have to be 20/20 after the fact, but it can be sought or gained beforehand. Your fate and/or impending doom can now be seen, managed, or controlled.

Why ask about their past? Well, because most women (not all) become intrigued, excited, or even mesmerized about many current qualities, skills, ✳and traits a man possesses. His body, penis, lips, eyes, beard, hands, feet, you name it. If you become so engulfed in those traits, your judgment may become clouded and your true intention may fade, especially if he's good at talking, along with these traits. A lot of men have the best gift wrapping and when you meet one with that "gift wrapping," your weakness becomes obvious and you begin to lose yourself! ✳

PEARLS

- Love me for who I am, not for what I have. For what I have has nothing to do with the love in who I am.

- As a true man, my mind is attracted to many things, however, I will adjust to the things that you don't have and become attracted to how you allow us to grow together.

- Don't ever be proud of being a bitch. If you are, you might as well be proud of one day becoming a widow.

- If you want to know who your real friends are, watch how people act when you; buy a new house, get married, buy a new car, renew your wedding vows, or get a bigger diamond ring.

- You want to control his money, you get mad about how he spends his money, yet, you make sure that he gives your mother money and nothing to his family.

- Don't ever disrespect your man and then treat your son like a king, they go hand-in-hand. If you do this, the upcoming king will have more respect for women who have no respect for men.

- If you only date sugar daddies, be prepared to help him with his sugar.

- There's a difference between "being in a relationship" and "investing in a relationship."

- Cast away your sins, then reel in your healing.

- Are you married and in a marriage or are you in a marriage and not married?

Chapter Six

When Nurturing Fails You

Lesson Two: The Attraction.

"Show me what-cha workin' wit'"

Women are naturally nurturing beings, more so than men. I'll give an instance which doesn't necessarily apply to all women. As a very successful woman; college-educated, healthy, with kids or none, a good credit score, clean driving record, and great family morals—once you meet or begin to date a man of lesser qualities, titles, a few things transpire.

Let's first talk about the woman who allows her titles or accomplishments to precede her. She'll open up in the beginning, either directly or indirectly. Indirectly, when her class becomes obvious, it pushes some men back on their heels. If a man doesn't possess what you have, it will show in his conversation, and body language. He'll become intimidated and start to look for your weakness. Since you were possibly sheltered as a kid, well-mannered, attended the best high school, and spent years in college, (or not), you'll tend to not recognize broken men, and therefore, won't know what to look for, i.e. *RED FLAGS*. Again, this type of woman has it all, she also possesses the ability to nurture, but she's missing important street knowledge.

Here is where both tables start to turn. He'll compliment you, make you smile, cater to your success, and inform you of what he doesn't have, compared to you. The man will make you think that you're in control, and at that time, the only thing you're in control of is your nurturing skills, which is what we want to be at the forefront. As men, we know this and lessen ourselves so that you now start to care, deeply. You're the type of woman that yearns for a family, he's not that type of man. This process may take some time but we don't mind, because the table has already begun to turn, shift. The table being your heart, mind, and nurturing skills begin to turn in our favor. You have been too busy with life to have enjoyed sex; mentioning this is a *bad choice*!

The process of nurturing is failing you now. He informs you about his life and you now think about rehabilitating him. You've already spent most of your life bettering yourself, making your parents proud, embracing a traditional lifestyle, and now it's time to celebrate. Time to share yourself. You owe it to yourself and the opportunity has arisen for him—the attitude of settling, for you. Finally, you can spread your wings, let your hair down, not knowing that you may be falling in love with an abuser, rapist, thief, whoremonger, narcissist, or psychopath.

I had narcissistic and psychopathic habits, but I mastered the whoremonger status. I paid for my first prostitute at age fifteen! The girls that I interacted with, at age fifteen, were interested in me, but paying for sex, in my mind, was satisfying. By paying, as weird as it sounds, I felt like I was helping a woman out financially. Honestly, because I was a child that always wanted to help my mother – and any woman for that matter – financially, I never knew which one felt better—the sex or giving her money! My mindset was that prostitution wasn't a crime because men were willing to pay, and the situation was similar to taking care of one's girlfriend like a provider. In my mind, it was similar to looking after one's own mother.

Mentioning your sex life, and what your ex didn't do or did wrong, can be detrimental, so be careful. Here's why it can be dangerous, in my experience.

It's ok to discuss these things because I think it's important that we both should have a playing field that's being manicured, not repaired. I must warn you about bringing up your ex. To me, that was the perfect time and opportunity to capitalize upon. I dove into what you were not getting as opposed to what I could provide.

When a woman realized that I was stunned about her sexual deprivation, the playing field automatically shifted to "Home Field Advantage!" Like I mentioned earlier, I've studied women to hurt them, not love them. I have read articles on their erogenous zones, where each zone is located, and how it feels to the woman. I've even tried areas that weren't mentioned in articles, and they work well too. Her body became mine!

Seize the opportunity.

Knowing a woman's body better than she does takes both of us to another level. For her, it's a whirlwind. For me, I have now regained control. All of your status, degrees, money, cars, and houses mean nothing to me. The importance of your accomplishments wears off. Your mind switches to thinking "What else can I do? I've done it all, except sharing my life (earnings, house, car, and your mind) with a man." You don't want to lose any of the lusters from working your butt off, but you don't want to lose me, either!

I'm the first and only guy that has taken the time to make great love to you, pay attention to the parts of your body that have been neglected for weeks, months, or even years. I am the first guy that isn't selfish, and you will *always* orgasm before I do. I can control it, just to control your mind!

Girl Talk:

"*Girrrrrrl*, I came before he did."

Now the downward spiral begins.

Nurturing is a great thing but you must be careful while doing it—sometimes it can work against you, even for the most polished woman! I want you to think that you're nursing me back to good health, a clear mind, but all the while, your habits are really working against you, because you feel

38

good about making me feel good, and not yourself! Women tend to finish what they start. I know this, so it's time for me to keep you committed to your word, unlike myself. How dare you *not* follow through, unlike me?

SOME WOMEN GO FROM NURTURE TO
NUDITY, AND AT THAT POINT, WE NUR-
TURE YOUR NATURE. ✳

~LEON R. WALKER JR~

Chapter Seven

The Protection

When Nurturing Doesn't Fail You.

Lesson Three: Nurture.

Nurturing is also paying close attention—being intuitive, not nosey when you are attracted to a man. You are your own investment. At this point, you've become aware of the little boy in your home and life—your man! I want to teach you how to protect yourself and see it before you read the next chapter which discusses what happens, or what could happen, if you don't see it when trying to pull away.

After the attraction occurs, and you've become aware of not only his antics, but his lack of morals, character, and integrity, you'll be ready to turn away. There will be many things that you will be attracted to, and you must know how to manage all of them. You will begin to struggle here though, and that's ok. While struggling, at least one part of it will be clear in your mind, and that is your protection.

Fear awakens people, and your self-preservation instincts can help you. Nature will intervene before the nurturing aspect. Your feelings and emotions are in a raw form, and I don't want you to read any further without your mind, emotions, and feelings being prepared. So, before you go into any relationship, you must be in the know. The same thing applies to reading about self-help. Consume it and change your life!

It's all about preparation. I'm not saying to go into a relationship and try to mother him. What I am saying is that you must be your own mother. I want to equip you to be able to deal with a man that you like but don't want, yet you are with him. Or the one you want to be with. Both types of men need nurturing, one needs to step it up, and the Bad Boy needs to step it down. You need to know about both types and how to manage them!

Lesson Four: Listen

I am not talking about listening with your ears here. A lot of times, you are too blinded by what you see to pay attention. It often happens when the penis takes prominence. When that occurs, you'll neglect many things and let them slide.

Let me change direction for just a moment. When a guy is well-endowed, your eyes are captured first, for the most part, then your hands. It's the feel, the touch, of a larger-sized man. For some of you, though, after the size is revealed, your mouth waters! At that moment, the excitement overwhelms you and you'll tend to forget about your other needs. You've waited for and wanted the "beatdown," to be stretched out, for far too long now. Then you get it, perhaps a few times, before you realize that he hasn't even taken the time to explore other parts of your body. Some well-endowed guys **will not** perform oral sex on you either!

You'll wake up when you realize that your clitoris or "G-spot" hasn't been stimulated in a while. Your "little lady in a hood" will pulsate, throb, and swell—even after he's finished! The magic wand is now just a wand! This doesn't always happen, but the larger-sized man will push right past your *G-spot* if he doesn't take the time to know your vagina!

Girl Talk:

"*Girrrrl*, now I need some damn lube. What's wrong with me?"

It's not you, it's him. It's you if you don't tell him, and if you don't convey your feelings, you'll end up with abrasions and swollen labia!

OK, back to what I was talking about.

Pay attention to your energy, your vibes, and frequencies. Your body will always talk to you, even before your mind catches on. Pay attention to the changes in smell in your house, car, sheets, everything. Listen with your eyes—*words* and *actions* go together or cancel each other out.

Words: For instance, what I mean by words is this: I will bring up a topic, one which I don't necessarily care about, just to engage you in conversation because I know you like to talk.

You'll ask me a question, and right after that, I'll do one of several things: answer you for the sake of it, give you an excuse, or avoid it by redirecting your question; anything to just get it over with. I'll even bring up something that I want to talk about, just to extend the conversation, yet you are still not satisfied because your question wasn't answered. You can feel my disconnection by *hearing* my answers and *seeing* my body language.

Actions: This is what I mean by actions: shopping for a birthday gift, a card, anything. Doing things together, I'm there physically, but I'm not present. It doesn't interest me.

You'll mention sex and I'll change, right in front of you. I will do things that suit me with more energy, and passion. For instance, I become very upbeat, friendly, and a tad bit more passionate when the topic of sex comes up. During this time, most, if not all, of my words will change. There will be eye contact, more discussion, up until sex is over with. You'll notice the switch in chemistry, from when you were trying to get me to talk, to bringing up sex. Only my chemistry will be present, not yours. Did you notice anything, here?

You should have noticed that I probably keep you around for sex only!

Sometimes you have to want the things you don't want—but need—more than the things you do want but don't need.

~ Leon R. Walker Jr~

PEARLS

- If you like her body, lick the whole thing.

- When you cum fast, you piss her off; this builds animosity.

- Use the toy with her. Don't be intimidated.

- Her butt cheeks are sensitive, they don't always have to be slapped. Make her stand while you kiss her ass.

- When performing oral sex, keep your teeth out of the way.

- Kiss her forehead every day.

- Play with her in public.

- Write a few words on the toilet paper.

- Always look up to her.

- Do not talk to his friends about him.

Chapter Eight

Step It Up—Mr. Nice Guy

Lesson Five: Content like Dad

By the time I had become Mr. Nice Guy, it was too late, I was a fake!

Mr. Nice Guy needs to open up. To you, he has great qualities, but he's boring. Marrying you was enough and it's on to the next phase of the marriage—lounge chair, ESPN. Keep in mind that you'll pay for the man-cave!

Sometimes, you meet a guy, just like you. You'll feel an attraction. It's refreshing at first, even breathtaking and fun. Men and women look for ✱ their parents in other people, but we often forget that different times breed different people! Emulation makes us comfortable; since our parents were married for fifty years, whatever dad did must have worked!

With this type of man, you don't have much to worry about. He's honest, faithful, a little caring, loves sex, but he's not manly enough. You respect his morals but not his swagger because he doesn't have it. He's become ✱ your son or even your brother and something just doesn't feel right. Sometimes you wish he would cheat so you can have a reason to unleash your inner freak—with someone else. Good boys don't last long.

You're really looking for that gritty, edgy person, the man who *lives life* on the edge, one who's spontaneous and with whom you're ready to engage in just a little bit of danger with. You've been a good girl all your life, so you'll try most things that he recommends.

On the other hand, the guy who is the same type of person as you becomes a bit boring. You have the same qualities, parents still married, kids/no kids, you have deeply profound morals—and this has felt like a life sentence to you. Don't get me wrong, these are all great qualities, but when you have lived *THAT* life already, you want more—or possibly, a little less—of a good guy!

You'll stick with the "nice" guy for a while, your parents like him, his parents like you. Maybe you all even discuss marriage, but in the back of your mind, after dating him for a while, your wild side begins to beg for an escape. Now, remember, you've buckled down for years, beginning in elementary school. After a nice glass or six of dry, red, sweet, white, dry--Sauvignon, Chardonnay, Pink Moscato, Pinot Grigio, or Sangria wine (all wines travel right to your vagina and its nerve endings) you tingle, constantly. You're chilling and feel quite sexy. One day you decide to ask Mr. Nice Guy:

"Babe, what do you think about toys in the bedroom?"

He pauses then smacks his lips—and that's all you need—*hmmmm!*

"Nah, we don't need any toys."

Your sex life just took a serious step *down* in your mind.

Then he goes back to doing what he was doing.

You sit on the couch, legs crossed because your vagina is pulsating. You gaze at the television, feeling rejected. Time to watch The *Ellen Show.*

But wait. You have one more question for him.

The wine warms your whole body. That "welcome home" peck on the cheek has gotten old! You haven't had a *deep, slow, passionate, warm, heart-rate increasing, tongue slashing kiss!*

"Babe, you haven't kissed me in a while."

"I know, I know. I've been tired from work."

"Hmph!"

You swirl your glass of wine, take a few sips, and an evil grin spreads across your face. You reminisce about the nice-looking cable, water, or any random maintenance man that comes by. Your fantasy kicks in while he's under your sink, working as you stare at his crotch.

Your mouth yearns for another tongue; you either have thought or often think about kissing a woman. You will kiss another woman to take the edge off. Be careful with this, though—other women know how to make a woman feel good. It's gotten to that point.

He really is a "good guy." Most of his friends are nerds, he speaks well, doesn't curse, and seems like the perfect guy. And maybe he is, but with each ticking moment, every now and then, your mind drifts off into your own fantasy world. Certain things you mention turn him off, making you want to be more and more uninhibited. Boredom slowly creeps in! The Cougar syndrome kicks in. Cougars have been neglected, so they're made! No one knows about your fantasy but you and your journal!

The Vulnerable Woman Girl Talk:

"Girl, Larry is nice and all. I like his dick, he's passionate too. He works his ass off, buys me nice things, helps with the kids. I just wish that one day, he'll come home and fuck the shit outta me!"

Your attrition is now building at an alarming rate! You begin to doubt your beauty and self-worth, and your focus shifts from the home and the work-place, to just wanting to climax!

Lesson Six: Step It Up

The Nice Guy can win, though. His morals are so strong, that he thinks of sex as something that only happens in the bedroom or when the kids aren't home, but it's minimal. For a woman that has a guy like this, if he can manage to overcome his upbringing (because that's what it is) you will have the damn near perfect guy. And it can be done.

You do this by slowly, and I DO MEAN SLOWLY, unraveling the inner workings of his "motherly" upbringing, both in thinking and instincts alike!

You'll have to undo what his mother taught him. Majority of the time—and this isn't taking anything away from the fathers—the mother has been the one teaching, showing, and grooming him to have high standards in a marriage. From the father, he'll get the talks about being tough, macho, working, taking care of the home, etc. Women carry family traditions, more so than men.

The Step It Up Guy has a mindset of thinking of sex-related things as "filth." A lot of "*Step It Up Men*" feel like everything is out of order, especially when one major physical thing is missing. His way of bringing you down off a limb is by pointing out that you have everything you need; however, he'll never mention *emotional support.*

Some, or most women, equate filth, or shall I say "nastiness," with being "uninhibited." A lot of times, this comes after her menstrual cycle.

Surely the wine puts her in a loving mood!

These men are also all about family and love, but never about "love-making." He not only has it confused but also totally separated. You have to teach him this during the "unraveling" session. His sex is basic, he orgasms once, always before you, then goes to sleep with a smile on his face, while you sit up, stare at him, imagine the cable guy, and play with yourself! Again you start to feel even more worthless and unattractive. The simplest things done by another man will turn you on. Vulnerability opens you up for *anything*! Sex novels turn you on, and love scenes in movies make you cry.

What he has to do is make sex a priority while putting his morals aside for a moment. In doing so, he'll notice things that he's been missing in you or reactions he has never known or seen. The "Step It Up Guy" is respectful and may be hesitant, even a little afraid, but he has an inner freak too. Being wound so tight, letting go will start to feel really good and natural to him, but you can't give it all to him, at once—take it easy. This is where his "Inner Little Boy" comes out to play. We all have one inside of us.

The "Step It Up Guy" is a work in progress. It's worth a try, but the "rewiring or unraveling" sessions are tough, especially when his mother still plays an active role in his life. Trust me, she'll notice what you're doing, and in most cases, she won't like it. At this point, it's not good to stay married for the kids or just because. You've tried counseling, talking with him one-on-one, spoken with his family, and nothing has worked. I'm not recommending divorce, not at all, but I am not saying to stick around and lose yourself and youth, either. Men need to receive reassuring confidence.

I highly recommend that you discuss his father and his relationship with his mother. There's a good chance that he was the same way and you can change that. It will take some time, but it works if he sees the issues and wants to become a better man for you. You have to know this for sure by asking the hard questions. This is when you need to make a decision, based on what he wants to do. If he agrees to show more attention among other things, then great. If not, that's his reply to the question of how much longer he's going to neglect you—it could be years. You are slowly becoming a neglected cougar—a made one!

WOMEN THAT DO NOT ASK ABOUT A
MAN'S DAD, COULD POSSIBLY SUFFER
LIKE HIS MOTHER!   *

~ LEON R. WALKER JR~

Chapter Nine

The Bad Boy

Lesson Seven: The Detraction.

Being with a Bad Boy, you can always fall back on your driven, successful self, your self before your self-destruction—because you will self-destruct, remember that. Even though you'll have a bout with the devil, God is in your locker room—the locker room being your foundation, morals, and open soul for your blessings to fall into. However, before you fall back into safety, you'll get what you asked for or fantasized about.

Girl Talk:

"Girrrrl, I got smart with him, he walked over to me, grabbed my hair and just had his way with me, he didn't even talk—and I couldn't even concentrate at work!"

Learn how to control yourself with or without him around. First, realize, know, believe, and understand that he will *only* do so much for you. Do not expect much else. The fun will be great but won't last for long, *at best, a solid six months*. If it lasts longer, then comes the time to take your worth away. Your experiences with him are extremely intense; you are enjoying your *"Bad Boy"*! In some cases, you've already given up some of your morals. You start to do things that you've never thought of doing—I'm not talking about good things either. In some cases, you experiment with weed, cocaine, sex outside in the car, in the garage, miss preparing the kids' lunch, finding excuses to miss games, meetings with school officials, and a host of other things.

Your instincts make you look through his phone and it gets worse. Being around women just like you makes you feel less than who you once were. Your insecurities are heightened in many ways. Depending on how long you remain with him, your looks fade, your glow declines, you start to lose weight and friends. The Bad Boy won't pay attention to your looks, hair, or make-up because he only wants what you offer—things to keep him well-fed, clothed, and money in his pocket. The other women, new ones, still have the fresh look, so that part, for him, is taken care of. You fall further and further down the back of his mental Rolodex!

Your credit cards are becoming maxed out. This man drives you to work and keeps your car, all day! In some ways, you feel like he balances you out. You explain this to your close friends, truly believing it. You advocate for him as well, although you know he's broken!

Many women have fallen victim to this *broken* man. That was who I once was. You know, I used to tell myself that I'll never take money from women, and I didn't. That made me feel good about what I was doing. However, I was taking their dignity, souls, hearts, minds, but most importantly—I took their innocent ways and morals—the same thing that was taken from me. I had held onto my anger since I was five. This man will do the same to you.

Reminder: At first, it was his looks, sex appeal, cologne, body—then the penis took over, and you let it!

I want you to think about this for a moment...

How do you allow something that doesn't have a brain to have so much power over you? Well, this is what I think: You've taken care of every aspect of your life and your career, however, you've neglected your vagina so much that it became needy. Your mind fell between your legs and the electric bullet not only became boring, but you also noticed that you aren't getting everything you need. A clitoral orgasm is good—really good and intense—but the feeling of a man's warm body, gripping his strong back and arms, pulling your legs back for him, grabbing his head while he performs oral sex on you, moaning, sweating, being pinned down, and choked just isn't there! After these thoughts resonate deep in your soul, you get mad at your vibrator! Some of you have thrown many away, then turned around to buy plenty more that are spread out and hidden all over the house.

Men like me have mommy issues. We don't like or want to be challenged. We respect the mentorship of men over women. I didn't have staying power or longevity in my relationships. Never go into a relationship with a man like me thinking it's going to last.

Like I mentioned earlier, you'll notice his need to take flight by *his motivation only being there when sex is mentioned*!

Take it one month at a time, because, after the third week, telltale signs of our abandonment will begin to show. The phone calls reduce, text messages aren't as juicy as they once were. Forgetting becomes the favorite word. We don't forget, we're just losing interest! You'll accept it but remember to take note. *We talk our way into your life while thinking of a way out*. For me, you were just a number!

All women catch our eyes because we're able to create her in our mind, even before sleeping with her. Cheating is fun and a challenge. We get off on women crying and being hurt. Getting off on seeing women cry and hurt is a way of suppressing our love for you. We're afraid of being hurt! Making up is easy; we come bearing gifts—and great sex!

Lesson Eight: Understanding Red Flags and Leaning In.

I'm powered up during sex and entertainment—that's it!

Ladies, you will end up with a Bad Boy if you don't ask about their past. I was literally a walking RED FLAG. What I'm about to tell you is the first and most important thing you need to do, understand, and make part of your life's plan in dating.

You can call it casual conversation, an interview, whatever, but it's essential and crucial that you *do not* talk about basic things. In the beginning, that's fine, however, you must get to the serious questions, sooner or later. Remember, Red Flags show either his true intentions, or future intentions, depending on how much he struggles with honesty or how easily he lies— both intentions expose a lack of power and also a plan to leave you soon, either physically or mentally. The sooner you realize this, the better prepared you'll be for his exit or your building with him. Always be gentle. Emotionally, you're in control.

If your conversation is basic and non-intrusive, you'll get basic and detached responses and engagement. One thing that's certain is that in my thirty-seven years of dating and relationships, there was never a time where we discussed Staying Power, or my past—*never*!

What is *"Staying Power,"* you might ask?

This definition is in my own words and isn't scripted, nor does it come from a dictionary. You need to know, wholeheartedly, what it is, but more importantly, where it derives from. I often mention my childhood and I will continue to. It's not that I haven't gotten over my childhood. I have; however, some men *never* do. They never do because they're afraid to confront and face it. I was, too. They're afraid of thinking or knowing the truth of possibly not being able to fix their past—there could be nothing further from the truth. If I can fix it, you can.

Staying Power.

✳ As a child, I had become deeply afraid of abandonment for many reasons. It started with my parents' divorce; that was the lens through which I also saw myself. I would become annoyed for whatever reason and instead of remaining committed in the relationship, I would run away. My father was told by the system to leave our home, and after leaving our home, he spent

✳ the rest of his life looking for a woman like my mother. I believe this is why men look for their mother in other women. The good mothers, that is. On the other hand, bad mothers—for whatever reason they weren't good mothers—just like bad fathers, leave an indelible mark on their sons— *pun intended*!

✳ Dysfunction in childhood causes men to become emotionally absent, afraid to love, insecure, guarded, detached, lost, and lacking knowledge of how to treat, respect, and flow with a woman. A man that loses or has lost his mother, for whatever reason, will rely solely on his manly and masculine traits, rendering him inept in his abilities to either know, do, or understand relationships—he simply can't relate!

I didn't have the power to stay; my power was in running away. In most cases, this can be reversed, but more often times than not, we'll use our childhoods as an excuse to remain our old selves, avoiding hurt, pain, and our ability to grow to love.

✳ Once a man feels like he can trust you, he'll share his past with you, so in the initial conversations, do not—and I repeat—do not pry too much. One way of getting a man to open up to you is to lead him into conversations concerning your past — this is called *Leading with your past.*

Psychological Reciprocity

Sharing and transparency build confidence and flowing exchanges, in both sexes. It makes men think and become comfortable. If he doesn't become closer to you after you have divulged certain flaws, he's not looking for a woman, relationship, or honesty; he just wants to use you. He's not ready to give you any part of him aside from his member, so be careful and aware of this.

Lesson Nine: The Conversation.

Just like most things, Red Flags are passed down! As men, we know when we have them, and the first thing we do when you mention it is get upset!

Women are more open with conversation than men. Use it to your advantage, positively. We are emotional, just like you. We cry, think, wonder, and harbor fears just like women do, but our masculine side pulls us back in like a magnet and predisposes us to repressing our emotions. This comes from our *"Shadow Traits."* I'll discuss this shortly.

To me, the most common mistake women make when meeting or dating a man is to disqualify the man right off the bat before they can evaluate and qualify him—this is why some women find themselves alone. Many women have idiosyncrasies, and we do too, yet they often feel like theirs aren't as bad as ours. Yes—you can take advice from your girlfriends, mom, dad, brother, friends, etc. Just remember that some of them are single, have never been married, are broken, jealous of you, and many more things. Some might just want the guy for themselves!

Lesson Ten: Of High Morals

The *Humbler* comes in many ways, fashions, and sizes. The Bad Boy has a reason and a season. Never will he be permanent; either he'll change, or he'll leave you *broken*!

Some of you have too much pride and expectations and refuse to relent or go against what you believe in. This will surely hurt you. I am not saying to settle or compromise in any way, no. However, there will be times when this inflexibility will be counterproductive, and here's why:

Sometimes, you'll need to swallow your pride. Remember, he might not be a good candidate—and neither are you—for some people or even a job. You can be and have been rejected, so remember where you come from.

Women with high standards forget one thing—they either worked their way up to this point or just naturally get it; either way, it took time and some of you forget that. Don't ever expect a man to have it all together all the time; it can be tasking. Holding high standards, you'll tend to look down on people and hold things against them. ✳

One thing is certain: women with this trait miss a lot of key points/lessons when they need to fall back on a man for protection. The more you make ✳ him feel insignificant, the less he'll be obliged to support and catch you. You are lacking in some areas, too. That's ok, as long as you know this and do not try to cover it up. Some areas you may be lacking in are: your street credibility/knowledge is probably extremely low, you've avoided the ghettos, unfamiliar people, and lack social awareness. Your understanding of people with issues is lacking, and you'll have a hard time relating to flaws and indiscretions.

I am not saying that you need to be hood or ghetto fabulous to have it all together, but it's crucial that you be very understanding of less fortunate ✳ people. If not, the fall from grace—the white picket fence, large house, and a loving husband—will be fast and hard, and it might be set in motion by your jealous girlfriend, the one you treat like crap, just like your man. Those two may find each other attractive!

Most times, when you meet people just like you—people who are always serious and strait-laced— you'll have one thing in common for certain:

a bit of unhappiness. Those who are just like you can help you with that because you'll see yourself in them. Take heed!

✳ Be grateful, humble, fair, and understanding. This will keep you grounded and emotionally safe from being devastated and/or letdown. The worst thing that can happen to a polished, sharp woman is to be used and abused by someone she's mistreated, put down and disregarded because of her ✳ wealth. It's not karma, it'll be a lesson. I was a loser at times, but you would not have noticed it from the outside, and plenty of times, I was sent to humble the Sadity! I wasn't your opposite attraction, I was your opponent. People come into your life for a reason or a season, most just… *Put On!* ✳

"YOU CAN'T FORCE PEOPLE TO RESPECT YOU, AND YOU SHOULDN'T RESPECT PEOPLE THAT FORCE YOU." ✳

~LEON R. WALKER JR~

PUTTING ON TO BE

Be real with me, instead of *putting on to be*.

You know, me being real with you,

you being fake with me, being someone you can't be, won't be,

not faithful.

It's silly, you see, *putting on to be*.

As real as I must be, socially, angrily,

you know that honestly, you can't be with me.

Probably because I'm too much for someone that has to *put on to be*.

Put on your manly ways or take off your weakest days, your sheep-

ish ways,

sneaky days, minimal pays, forgotten praise, it all comes out.

When you put on to be, you know those qualities that I can see,

that you can't see, freely trying to be, someone you can't be.

Like the man that really wants me, because you are too busy *putting on*

to be.

Let's Talk - Bad Boys, more often than not, try to impress women from the start. We often forget that women, for the most part, will and have accepted us for who we are. Yet we change, thinking that we have to be someone that they want, when in reality, all they want is a genuine, honest, truthful, and sincere man, even if he is **broken**! Those are the qualities that they eventually grow to want.

However, in our growth, depending on our environment, we normally grow away from our natural path. Dysfunction becomes natural to us. That **broken** man, like myself, clearly hasn't dealt with his own Shadow Traits and Behavior

A Shadow Behavior is a negative and most times, automatic, unintentional, and unconscious response to things, events, people, and situations. We all exhibit different Shadow Behaviors. Some may act differently, resist change, manipulate people, or behave aggressively.

PEARLS

- Rub her scalp.

- Paint her nails.

- Know your role. Be the woman, and the woman only

- When you introduce her to other women, kiss her.

- Always consult him or her about everything

- Don't tell him what to do; make suggestions without wanting or needing him to always take them.

- Pay for his massage.

- Just leave him alone for one or two days a week.

- If you want soft lips on your penis, remember, she wants soft lips on her clit, vulva, and the labia too.

- Don't push her head down on you, let her enjoy herself trying to take it all. She wants to, anyway, because she knows what we want.

Chapter Ten

Numbers

If you're only enamored with penis size, you'll always be lonely because ✳ that's all you'll get. Men are pleased with you being that way. You're very easy to please as long as we measure up! I have yet to meet a woman who asked about my numbers. Yes, credit scores are important, but many other essential numbers are in a person's life. I have had more than a million conversations about many things with people, yet my numbers still haven't come up. However, when I ask a woman about her numbers, she's taken aback. These numbers play a significant role in all relationships, households, raising children, etc. They can hurt, derail, sidetrack, set you back, extend your life, or possibly even kill you. Once you know them, you may be able to save your own life. Reading further, I talk about many numbers and the importance of them.

Real conversation:

"So, how tall are you, and how much do you weigh?"

"I'm five feet, nine inches tall, and I weigh 220 pounds."

"Hmph—you're a thick guy, huh?"

"Yeah, I am."

"I like thick dudes!"

Soon after, a date was made. We proceeded to friendship and then sex! This is how many conversations go when people first meet. Once you begin to like him, your vision and judgment become clouded. Many times, ✳ women are concerned about a man's height and weight. Either he's too short, too tall, too heavy, not heavy enough, not tall enough, and many other things. They can't wait to know about his penis size, as mentioned previously, another critical number for many women. Physical numbers are not the only measurements you should know about someone.

Real conversation and event:

"Sheila, Leon had a heart attack! He's been rushed to the hospital—they're operating on him right now!"

I remained in the hospital for one week after the surgery. Then, I began rehabilitation, which lasted for six months. At the time of my heart attack, I was pretty fit and exercising every day. In fact, the heart attack started at the gym. I had no clue it was building up to take me out! After leaving the gym, I walked to my car, chest burning, drove to the track on base, walked for a moment, drank some water, and still didn't feel any better.

I then drove myself and walked about fifty yards into the hospital emergency room. This is where my life changed. They conducted an EKG, determining that I was having a heart attack and rushed me into emergency surgery. My cholesterol levels were through the roof; my blood sugar levels were also dangerously high. My arteries were eighty-percent clogged.

Dr. Shimansky, my cardiologist, spoke to me on the operating bed. I was semi-conscientious.

"Mr. Walker, had you arrived fifteen minutes later, you would have died. Luckily, you are in good shape, and you were blessed to be able to walk into the hospital."

"Doc, before I walked in the hospital, I drove across the base—my chest was burning then, and I was sweating profusely."

"From the looks of it, your heart attack started a while ago. Presumably, it continued while you were driving."

At the time, my girlfriend had no clue about my numbers, any of them—blood sugar, cholesterol, vitamin D levels—and we had been together for five years. My health numbers were never discussed, and neither was hers. I mention this because, as we know, men do not see their physicians regularly enough for checkups. Some women are good at asking these questions, but most are not. Married women tend to be more concerned about their husbands' health since illness can impact the entire family. Aside from knowing or asking him about his numbers, you must also be aware of his genetics. The men in my family have suffered from heart attacks, high blood pressure, diabetes, low vitamin D levels, and other health conditions. You need to know his health background, *his numbers*! What if his eyesight starts to decline six months after you get married, and he goes blind? How will this affect you and your children? How about losing a finger, hand, or even his right leg, the driving leg? What if I was driving with my woman, her son, and my kids at a speed of 75 MPH and had a heart attack? I was driving on the Naval Great Lakes base while having a heart attack!

Lesson Ten: Learn their numbers

Discuss his and your numbers, and be honest, not embarrassed about it. Don't get me wrong, either genetically or if your partner just likes a bigger size, both of you must manage your health. If they want to lose weight, due to wanting to enjoy a more prolonged bliss and eternal life with you, help them. Either way, your partner can still be healthy as your Big daddy, Big Shawp, Big Poppa, Big Momma, or just Momma/Daddy!

Your numbers are tied to your financial stability. The next set of numbers to discuss, especially for military men, is his life insurance. It's not all about how much you'll get when or if he/she dies. It's about who's in your will, and for military personnel, specifically, the Navy, who's on your page two.

Real conversation:

"Master Chief Walker, we have a possible suicide."

My senior leader informs me that at a specific location, there may be a gentleman who has been burned to death. We look into the situation and find that, sadly, he was dead—he burned from the inside out, within his home.

What does this have to do with numbers, you might ask? Well, it has to do with the number "2," as on page two—the document that outlines our beneficiaries, which I mentioned earlier. During the investigation my leaders and I must conduct, we were required to ask about the "PNOK," Primary Next of Kin. In most cases, it's the spouse, but not always. The gentleman who killed himself was divorced and remarried but never changed his PNOK from his past wife to his current wife. After closing the case, we discovered his ex-wife was legally entitled to his insurance policy. She was to receive $400,000.00! So, what do you know about your partner's page two?

There are other numbers that you should be concerned with, and those are credit scores. However, more importantly, is the credit report and its contents. Does your significant other excessively take out loans? Has his or her property been repossessed? Is there an abundance of late payments and revolving credit? It is easy to read the credit reports, but are you aware that your partner's debt becomes yours once you are married, and vice versa? Creditors derive your credit score by examining how well you repay what you have borrowed. If they can't repay companies, what makes you think they'll repay you? The report, in my opinion, is a great measuring stick of character and integrity. Be aware of what property you are about to inherit—it's called marital property!

Become familiar with the hidden numbers, or numbers that are not—but should be—obvious. Following my heart attack, I learned my dental health is just as important as anything else. Broken teeth, root canals, and teeth that haven't been professionally cleaned can also affect the heart. How often does your partner see the dentist? Bad teeth or poor dental hygiene can cause bad breath, further leading to them not wanting to kiss, leading to sexual neglect.

Earlier, I mentioned height, weight, and penis size; however, other numbers will affect penis/vaginal functionality, leading to more sexual neglect! For instance, financial stress will affect sex drive, loving emotions, and the ability to extend the attention you want, require, or desire from your partner. More attention will be placed on bills and what cannot be purchased for you and the kids. Financial stress can also lead to a sedentary lifestyle and bad eating habits, leading to a potbelly (gained weight). I developed a gut, too. I'm not saying this type of stress alone will cause all of the already stated issues. Please be aware that we'll blame our present stress on our job to avoid being embarrassed about not having our finances in order. My bosses never caused me that much anxiety, but being broke did!

Now, back to his height. You may wonder why I mentioned stature. Well, you will notice that if he's not standing tall, he'll seem shorter, of course, which is related to bad posture. The reason for his bad posture, rounded shoulders, equating to a lowered head (which makes him seem shorter) is an evident lack of confidence. He thinks that he can't provide financially, causing an appearance of "slumping over," and not wanting to look you in the eye. Other clues to be aware of are short answers, or possibly no answers, consistent frowning, avoidance of discussing costs, holidays, or even gifts, increased smoking and alcohol habits, and a change in appetite, resulting in drastic weight loss or weight gain. As the financial woes magnify, you may notice his lengthened deep thoughts, a shunning attitude, cold-shouldering, refusal to open bills, blanking, being overly lethargic, and looking past you, which can, and will happen, anywhere. Women experience financial stressors, too, the same as men. A woman's behaviors are different from men, though. Things to cast a wide net for are changes in her menstrual cycle, hair loss, binge eating, reduced spa treatments, her bodily secretions will subside, and a loss of motivation and enthusiasm. Some women even stop going to or lessen their appearance at church!

One hard-to-notice, covert, and major coverup that men miss is that women will increase the amount of foundation they wear during their financial issues. Some men don't know much about foundation because we're more enamored with lipstick or lip gloss like I was, and this is why it's hard to detect. It's not only about not feeling pretty, but not feeling like they are not executing their part, financially. Mentally, their application of foundation is no longer make-up, but it is now a mask! A lot of verbally and physically abused women wear foundation, too. Later in my book, I discuss abuse in the "types" chapter, so please do not think that it was overlooked. It wasn't. Abuse was not put on the back-burner. Yes, physical, mental, sexual, and spiritual abuse are all very much worth discussing, and we will. They are very sensitive and extremely important topics. I am a staunch advocate in reducing all forms of abuse; it's my passion. At this time, I want to stay consistent with the "numbers" portion.

As core-beings, what we must come to know and believe is that those that genuinely care will do what they have to, to make ends meet, regardless of any deficit concerning money. If you are alone in the "lack of finance" world, most other things in the relationship will suffer. When one partner puts financial distractions above everything else, it will lead to loneliness. Having a good and wealthy core--the core being all above money-- breeds real spiritual confidence. Genuine, spiritual faith is called "weallthy". Yes, I spelled it with two 'L's" and here's why

WEALLTHY= YET, LET, WE, HE, THY, ALL, HEAL, EAT. However, you want to arrange it!

Now, onto the last, but deeply alarming, filthy, and trifling, topic concerning my street finances (numbers). I was a man that liked to paint the town red! Some people call it "splurging;" others may call it "caking" or "spend master." You name it, and I did it. With that, money came and went on liquor but mainly on women. As I matured, I came to realize that I didn't have to spend all of the money that I did on hotels, motels, getting car seats detailed, indecent exposure tickets, damaged car hoods, damaged trunks, broken stilettos, scuffed Louboutin's, newly done acrylics, hairdo's, trips to the cleaners, etc,--all I had to do was be honest and patient. As you have read and can clearly see, my galavanting was tied to other women, which is why I combine women and finances in this chapter. To no fault of theirs, citing the sinful, vile, and nefarious little boy that I was, (while being a financial giver in an unmannerly state of mind, and for the wrong reasons--my selfish ways), my judgment was clouded. I misled women and lied to them. I wasted their time and gave them false hope, but more importantly, I could not be blessed in their presence. Nor could they be blessed, while with me. My women may have been covered, but what good is it to be partially covered? That was my fault, in that my inept possession of procuring proper principals kept the two of us in clear and present danger. My covering was unheeded! During that time, and I truly believe this, now, my spirit and soul were shut off to God, and widely open to the devil. I knew better, and that too was my choice. When your soul and spirit are turned away from God, blessings will not enter your body. They will remain within reach because God is forgiving, but you must do your part, and I didn't--I WAS TIED! All of this relates to "unheralded communication." Honest and soul-cleansing communication, due to my fears and abhorrent knowledge of "Broken Self," was not extended to any woman. It was unfair. This leads me to conclude this discussion and pose a profound, dark, and spine-chilling question? For me, and I would gather for others who have apprehensions about my next question and number.

A very heavy number, and one that I think, supersedes all because it is in conjunction with other people and their inner demons. Have you asked about their soul-ties or sex demons? What about their sex numbers? Sadly, mine was pretty high! I will forever have to live with that embarrassment. Gangsters, and you'll hear it in rap songs, for reasons other than what I am discussing, call it "Body Count." What's your partner's Body Count? Those ties, demons, and residual body counts just might enter your body/ spirit, too.

I've heard women say:

"Girl... I don't even want to know, so far...we're good!"

Then, she walks right into the bedroom with a group of demons--myself included! A sex-demon, or a sex-tie, will do many things. It will cause you to call someone else another person's name. It could also make you perform positions or desire different things with your partner, something that you've never done before. That was my experience. It could happen many times. To put you at great ease, and if you have these ties, bodies, and demons that I had, I will share a true story with you before we continue, that will surely help you. I, too, was afraid, shocked, and taken aback when I learned about soul-ties. First, it's never too late to reverse them. If you don't know about them, learn. If you don't believe they exist, do your research. Either way, have plans to exterminate the negative soul ties. According to the Bible, the term soul ties, is referred to as a "knitting together," becoming one flesh.

I met my dear friend, Agape, on Facebook. A beautiful, genuine, honest, and God-fearing woman. She asked me one day. Leon, do you know what a "soul-tie" is?

"No, I don't, what are they or what is it?"

"Listen, you need to learn about them, Leon, I see the lord is working with you, and soul-ties are a part of your new journey!"

"I'm afraid, a little, Agape, but you're right, I need to learn and digest them." Thank you, Agape, much appreciated, I'll start tonight. This will be a soul cleansing for me, one that's much needed. From now on, it is my quest to open up more and be honest about my past.

This conversation took place last year and has been very eye-opening for me, and it will be for you as well.

A soul tie is a physical connection between two people. It comes when two people have been intimate. It has also been known to form after an *intense* spiritual or emotional relationship. These can also make you a better person, by providing strength and support. Some are negative as well. Either way, if you plan to reverse the negative soul tie, you must avoid the person and ask God for strength to move on. When you repent, stay the course! I tried repenting, several times, but didn't know what I was doing, nor did I take it seriously. Had I known about soul ties years ago, I would have failed at turning away from them, miserably. Honest repenting is required when it's a sinful soul tie. You must also remember, that, unclean spirits can feed off of one another, herein lies a *demonic influence*. I possessed a demonic influence for years, so much that I had embodied it and became extremely comfortable with it. The demons became my norm, therefore whomever I was with, were imminently doomed! For years I struggled with good and evil! Because of that, fornication, deception, lying, cheating, and being promiscuous, didn't mean anything to me. My demons needed to be fed, not my morals. I was as rotten as can be. So I know, whichever force you feed, that's who you become. Back then, if my soul had a face, I'd easily appear as the devil! God had me all along, though, but I did feel bad because I knew better, and I didn't accept or have him, yet he never forsake me.

Discussing "soul-ties" has to become a part of your *relationship components*, which we'll get into next.

"DON'T EVER FEEL BAD ABOUT NOT
KNOWING SOMETHING. FEEL BAD FOR
NOT WANTING TO KNOW SOMETHING."

~ LEON R. WALKER JR~

Chapter Eleven

Components of a Relationship

There are many components of a relationship that must be discussed, well-thought-out, worked on, and implemented. I, too, learned them at age fifty, when I attended and completed six months of therapy. Before my therapy however, I hardly ever spoke about these components. I'll list the ones that I learned and read about. There are many more, which you should also discuss with him and implement.

- Do you know his parents and their past?
- Does he know your parents and their past?
- Who will do what chores in the house and will you all rotate those chores?
- What do you like, want, need, and desire?
- What does he like, want, need, and desire?
- Who has triggers and what are they?
- Can you discipline his kids?
- Can he discipline yours?
- Where is your point of mutual balance and how do you both get to that point?
- Are you both adjusting to what your parents passed down, both negative and positive?
- What makes both of you happy or sad?
- Are either or both of you romantic or intimate?
- Which parent do you not talk to or like—and why?
- Do you have any mental blocks?

- What are your fears?

- Do you have any sexual fears?

The above mentioned components should prompt open dialogue about many events and occurrences. For instance, speaking of mental blocks, I had a major mental block that affected me sexually, and not one woman knew about it because we took turns just talking instead of having open communication with each other. Speaking about traumatic events, such as a childhood molestation can be quite scary, however, doing so now, has taught me that women respect you more for your transparency. Years back, I didn't feel safe enough to be open about it, so they never found out. I had trust issues, and a communication barrier, not because of them, but because I didn't trust myself. I felt that if I was open about my past, she may have laughed at me, or left me alone, therefore opening up my anger issues, so instead of being honest, I held it inside. Thinking back on it now, I should have given her the option to learn more about me, or at best, help me open up, which women are very good at. My communication barrier could have been removed, years ago!

I was molested and raped by family members and each time they did, their first order was to tell me to be quiet or cover my mouth with their dirty hands and fingers, during the molestation and after. Eventually and having *not* processed the act of silencing, I became a very quiet man during sex! There were tons of times when a woman had to ask me *"Leon, did you cum?"*

I would always put my head down in shame, knowing that I did enjoy her, but I could never express it verbally!

Therefore, it is important to learn, discuss and implement these facets or *components of a relationship* in order to truly know and understand your partner as well as improve and sustain your relationship. Being verbal in bed, not only makes her feel good, but a woman wants to know if she's pleasing you. The more you moan and talk, the more she'll be inclined to do!

PEARLS

- Hump her—just because.

- Make her a "Honey-do" list—just special things that she likes, for her to search for.

- If you don't respect each other, go your separate ways, amicably. ✶ Don't hold on to someone that someone else can love, like, and appreciate. ✶

- Whoever is boring in the relationship has given up.

- Loving your kids is different from loving him.

- While out, leave your phones in a purse or face-down on the table.

- Love us like you would love a big baby; we're grown, but we also want to let go sometimes.

- Always look into her eyes when talking to her.

- When you have an orgasm, kiss her deeply. Don't pull away. Then look into her eyes.

- Meet her at the door when she comes home from anywhere. It immediately makes her day or evening even better.

Chapter Twelve

Communication

I inherited a personality of addictiveness and extremeness from my parents that played out in my life in various ways. For many years, I used these my personalities in the wrong ways, manners, and fashion.

Had I employed the proper communication skills in any way, my life, and that of my partner, would have been much better. I would have even revealed my dark secrets to her. A man would be able to convey certain things to a woman, and vice versa, if he trusts her.

Like I mentioned earlier in the book, my method of communicating and building trust is by "Presenting My Past." This means being extremely open, honest, and transparent about myself, my intentions, but most importantly, my past, and how I am now walking in it with a different mindset!

Am I past my past or is my past still my present, including the other women that were in my past? These are things that women want to know, especially if it concerns another woman. Not that she's intimidated at all, but a woman wants to know if the woman in your past still has her hooks in you, exists, has an effect on you, or doesn't mean anything to you. This includes the mother of your children or someone that may have had an abortion for you!

✗ Some exes have a hard time letting go and will go to any length to disrupt or destroy what her ex-man currently has going on with you, his new lady. She'll lie, keep the kids away from him, even go to extreme lengths to find out how much he gets paid so she can increase child support in an effort to reduce your quality of life with him.

Another thing she'll do is remain close to his family. Acts of kindness such as dropping the kids off with his parents or siblings are done with the intention of remaining close to him, not his family. This is her attempt to leverage closeness and continue to groom feelings and engage in conversations with his family, so that they will continue to see her in a good light, regardless of her predatory ways, and continue to invite her to family functions. While she's over there at family functions with his family, she'll have her eye on both of you, collecting information. Collecting information is a means of measuring and comparing herself against and to you.

In this situation, the best thing for you to do is to remain supportive and silent, with reference to responding to the ex. What the *Ex* really wants is to disturb you emotionally so that your desires to please him become secondary. She'll attempt to get in your head, telling you things that he has said or done and the promises he's made that you've seen and experienced as well. There may be some truth to it, but the obvious fact remains that you and she are different in many ways—and that's why he'll remain and build with you, and not her.

No, he isn't perfect and she may have had certain triggers for him or he may have had triggers for her, which created toxins in their previous relationship—either way, it'll be hard to dismiss her as "just another stalking ex." So don't be in a hurry to ignore her, but manage your feelings, emotions, and thought processes in order not to take sides or rush to judgment quickly. She wants to be at the forefront of *your* mind, not his. Don't allow her to rent space in your head, relationship, or home life. Some women and men spend an extraordinary amount of time and energy on revenge and being vindictive, even at the cost of other people—you or his children!

You should also try to continue to keep him happy and looking good. In some cases, this will deter her, but in other cases, it will make her even more upset and she'll intensify her intrusive spying and attacks. At this time, you'll have to make it official—legally. Make sure you believe your man before you believe a scorned ex. They can be very manipulative, deceptive, cunning, and persuasive.

However, just for good measure, your man has to be honest about everything pertaining to his ex. Many times, her actions, behaviors, and reactions are a direct reflection of how he misled, lied to, or tricked her. I've done this on many occasions. I found that the "ex" just wants an apology for all of the man's wrongdoings, and only acts this way so she can have closure. If you all plan to move forward with and engage in an open, honest, fruitful, and healthy relationship, I think that it is not only crucial but also essential to have a safe meeting of the minds. Doing so will create and develop many things, including trust and clarity. Since you can remember and document everything he's told you, his story will begin to make sense.

Lesson Twelve: Comms Down.

In the Navy, when "comms" (communications) are down, a ship can be rendered useless, defenseless, Dead in the Water (DIW), and in trouble on all fronts. The same thing goes for a relationship.

Communicating rules all and here's why. Starting off as friends with open dialogue, communication builds our foundation or determines if we'll even have a foundation, an attraction, things in common, and if we'll be a good fit or not. If a man doesn't talk in the beginning stages, it will not change much later. He's either just a quiet guy, *which drives women crazy*, has ulterior motives and is processing them as you speak, or simply doesn't have much to say. Men that don't have much to say will sometimes not have much to offer, such as things that feed your spirit, your soul, powerful and well-thought-out words.

I learned that the smallest thing(s) can touch a woman's heart. It starts with

"What You Remember." Women could care less about material things— they want facts, openness, truth, honesty, a great listener, and to be chal- lenged mentally, in a healthy way.

What You Remember means a lot to her.

When you challenge a woman mentally (talking about, responding and referring to her favorite color, food, dish, shoe, perfume, etc. that she spoke about, early in the relationship) many things occur for both of you. For you, you'll receive the nice things; the good attitude, compliments, absence of pressure, but more importantly, her body will react sexually, sensually. In many ways, it can be new to you and her. New to her because she has either never been so taken care of mentally, or has refused to com- pletely open up, because of her past. This does not mean that a good man is one who does the things listed above for a woman, but a man that's in tune with his "feminine side," the side that allows him to understand a woman just as much as he understands himself!

In most cases, women like to talk, receive reciprocity, and know that you are into her at their level or a level conducive to growth and develop- ment. Men that don't talk much, respond to your questions, give advice or exchange ideas don't see any value in your knowledge, expressive ways, or your yearning to be heard, celebrated, respected, and admired. As a man, becoming capable and showing these qualities would come easy when she respects you and your brutal honesty. This goes for the silent man too; he's probably silent because of his past, either as a result of being mistreated as a child, left behind, cheated on, and ignored, or is ignorant about how his silence hurts her. Women want to be in the know, not to be nosey but to offer help.

For many years, I found it hard to tell a woman "Baby I don't know," "I can't do that," "I'm confused," etc. However, after completely purging arrogance, cockiness, shame, secrets, and selfishness from my mind, body, and soul, I found that women will accept you, not just for who you are, but for your potential to be a greater man. All this comes from not only your aforementioned *brutal honesty* but a healthy aura!

One of the most beautiful things that transformed me from the inside was my "brutal honesty." It has been extremely liberating, opening myself up to cleanse my soul and spirit, and to also welcome true love with someone who will not judge me. A person that resonates with one's aura will not judge you because they *see you before they hear you!* Your cleansing will resonate through your smile, a confident gait, nice gestures, and radiance—your aura precedes! Healthy auras can help lower a person's guard.

You may wonder why I mentioned the aura? Well, this is because I have experienced it even before I knew what it was. I have seen dark, light, and pretty auras illuminate from my body at certain times. I also noticed that depending on the color, if I didn't exercise caution at that moment, many things, although correctable, occurred. If you don't take heed, you'll take that same negative energy into all of your future relationships. You'll even become stagnant in your current relationship.

In addition to the aura, you may want to know your *Visual Cortex* so that you can become engulfed in your *visual stimuli*! You'll know it when your body becomes warm and tingly! Having or knowing these traits, understanding, engaging, relating with, and responding to any human becomes enlightening for both. However, you must communicate your interest, knowledge, or experience with Auras and a Visual Cortex—talk about them! If neither of you has experienced this, then this is a great time to talk about it over coffee, feeding the ducks, or sometime before or during lovemaking. Some women are left cold, and you'll definitely know if this happens!

One's aura cannot be hidden. If you look for it or become familiar with *auras,* your vision will save you time, protect your heart, feelings and forestall any future thoughts of giving someone with a dull aura a chance.

Just keep in mind, like my aura, and the dull appearance I presented, you can also see, feel, and hear an aura that's in its growing stages. When connecting with a person that's truly on their way up, with reference to change and transparency, energy levels coincide, become upbeat, circuits interact, flow, and travel in sync! New ideas arise, too. This new or old couple becomes inseparable, and it's possible that the man just needs to *remember* the old and the new and be willing to be *taught to communicate.*

WE ALL HAVE ONLY ONE MOUTH. SADLY, SOME PEOPLE USE THAT ONE MOUTH FOR ONLY ONE THING!

~ LEON R. WALKER JR~

What I Remember

I remember what you told me,
so later you don't have to scold me, mold me,
but hold me when I remember what you told me.
I remember what he did to you,
what he said to you, that changed you, for me.
Now let's see, it was he who forgot,
or what not—not me—but you treat me like him,
and see me like him, but you need to remember
that I remember that he didn't remember.
I'm not him.

Let's Talk – Women remember almost everything, especially the things they ask or request for. Sometimes, it's a test to see if we're listening. It's very important, as a man, to remember the small things like the first day you met, the location, what she wore, how she smelled, her favorite place to go, the nail color she wore that day, ring size, amongst others. These are indicators of a man's sensory perception skills, if he has them, or not!

They're especially important, and she will ask you again, sometime later, as the relationship progresses. You should mention these first and make sure to jot them down.

There's one thing that is certain to help a man, and that is knowing her menstrual cycle. Remembering this can give you a head start on things that may bother her. In the beginning, women *will not* discuss this. Some will, but most won't. If she doesn't, it's up to you to notice, and if she does, take notes and pay attention. During this time, some women are very emotional, desire chocolate, desire to be held, want peace and quiet, or will sleep often. Be very observant each day. Don't be afraid to buy tampons either, or whichever one she wears. DO NOT come home with the wrong ones! Also, never ask her about her weight during this time, never do it at any time, and certainly not during her cycle!

TEACH ME

Teach me how to love you in a special way,
your way can then become our way, for that special day.
I will teach you how to care for my delicate ways,
my delicate heart, my wanting to stay, and not run away.
You need to know me, I need to show you,
how willing I am to go through tough times,
hard times, better times,
grow through your old pains, suffering, and doubts
to show you that you can reach me by wanting to teach me.

Let's Talk - Don't ever be afraid to be led by a woman. When she takes control or takes over, there's no need to feel insignificant; at that moment, she just might have a better idea in mind. They have their ways and we have ours, but for the most part, women want a man to be in front but one that won't mind taking a backseat every now and then.

Women enjoy surprises but what they enjoy more than anything is surprising us. Letting her take the lead on occasion makes her feel trustworthy. She definitely doesn't want to feel like her son is more mature than you! Teaching you is also a way of letting you know that she's interested in moving forward; most women will not do this if they don't see any return on their investment. If she starts to ask about the great examples of men in your life, this is her way of telling you that you need to take notes from them. Be smart and do so; she's either making an exit plan or still trying to build with you. Don't take it personally and she'll be patient, but you must show growth.

CONVERSATION

Talk to me, let me hear your soul through your whole being.

Talk to me baby, connect with me.

When we talk, I hear you, I feel you,

when we talk, I connect with you.

I get to know you, soul you, then hold you.

Your words sit with me, when you talk to me,

when I walk, you see, your words stay with me.

If you talk to me, you will have no worry,

your words move me, groove me, soothe me.

Talk to me, baby, could it be that when you talk to me,

I can hardly breathe. It's more than satisfactory,

more than you and me.

All you have to do is talk to me, he will see then,

how you cherish me.

Let's not take turns talking, that's not communicating with me,

that's talking down to me,

uplift me, all you have to do is, talk to me.

I want to understand you, grow with you,

express your ways, I'll express mine.

See? It's that easy,

When we talk, our hearts become intertwined.

Your heart beats, just like mine. The more you talk,

the more I find that deeper grind. That talking,

your line, comes to me, it pulls me in

closer to you, when only you talk like you do.

It keeps me safe, happy, and wanting to please you.

Just talk to me. I know what you want, that penetration,

yeah I know what you want, but that penetration,

brings my hesitation, until you have that conversation.

Baby, just talk to me.

Let's Talk- The art of talking has been lost. Words mean a lot; they can be gratifying, satisfying, horrifying, or in some cases, mortifying. They don't have to be because we choose our words, and as men, most times, we don't do it wisely—I know I didn't. There should be a natural flow to communicating and not "taking turns" talking—there's a big difference.

If you have things in common, are great listeners, and are feeling each other, it will show in the conversation. Don't be in a rush to tell her what you have and what you can do. You must feel each other out but don't make it too obvious, we both know what's going on here. Also, during the conversation, it's not healthy to mention The Ex. This is one thing that will turn both of you completely off. Regardless of whether it's negative or not, The Exes remain where they are, as Exes! Bragging is also a major no-no. You want to leave some things to the imagination. Never discuss sex in the first few meetings or in some cases, the first few months. Women respect a man more if he's not all about sex, but more interested in knowing her, and her kids, if she has any. Don't complain and never put anyone down— being prejudiced sends red flags!

Try your best not to act like you're her teacher like when you jump the gun to answer her question before she finishes asking it. Doing a "data dump" on her can ruin the conversation, too. Knowing when to be quiet is a good thing. Leave your job right where it is, don't bring it to the dinner table. For the women who like to talk a lot, this can be a really bad thing, and I do mean really bad! Work on this because you can really make a man do some of the following things when you are very talkative. He could shut down, doze off, end the date early, avoid your phone calls, or make up things in order not to date you again. Women that are either in a relationship or are coming out of one with a quiet man suffer from wanting and needing to just talk, express herself, or in a lot of instances, find answers. Always express yourself but *DO NOT* dump on anyone and make it just about you!

Chapter Thirteen

Two Crucial Crucibles

Aside from everything that I discuss in Loveship, I would like to extend to you what I consider two significant and powerful crucibles concerning your partner. It applies to both men and women. The science of it is interchangeable. Let's consider the topic of sports. Throughout my thirty-two years in the Navy, and now, five years post-retirement, I continue to hear many women not understanding why we love sports. I'm not going to explain our love of sports; however, I will tell you that it's an important time for us. There are three to four days that we become entrenched in sports. The most popular days for games to be broadcast are Saturday, Sunday, Monday, or Thursday. Football, hockey, golf, rodeo, baseball, tennis, golf, boxing, UFC, college football, track and field, swimming, etc; you get my point. Please pay close attention to this, especially those who don't believe in sports, put education over sports (I highly agree), or aren't into sports. If you don't want to learn about a particular sport, that's fine, but it's very important to know what your partner likes about sports. We enjoy at least three to four uninterrupted hours on the above-mentioned days. That does not mean that you shouldn't or cannot be around us. You should be during that time, which actually makes it better. Try to refrain from continually going to your friend's house. Doing so shows avoidance. Maybe she and her husband have the same issue, and sometimes the wives discuss this while they visit one another then return home pissed off!

Here are my recommendations.

CRUCIBLE NUMBER ONE: Games or a series on television

- Help with pregame shopping.

- Invite your friends over for drinks and an activity in a different room.

- Help with serving snacks.

- Wear a sexy jersey of his favorite team or even a hat. This is a winner!

- Stay away from being in front of the television.

- Make a list of sports that are coming on or upcoming in the future.

- Pay for a special pay-per-view event.

- Plan half-time activities.

- Hug him now and then, even a friendly quick peck on the cheek or forehead, and walk away.

- Walk by and rub his head.

- Try to put the kids to sleep early or plan to keep them occupied.

- Participate in being a host, then do your own thing-- just take part, even for a short period of time.

- Plan for designated drivers.

- Plan ahead for possible sleepovers. One thing for sure is that men love when our spouses are supportive of friends staying over. I know we have to be careful with this, but try your best not to be totally against it.

- Don't get pissed off about the noise and trash at the end of the night, but be aware of it.

- Invite your neighbors.

- Try your best to minimize any discussions unless it's needed or required at the time.

- Smile and be social. The worst thing you could do is let anger or disgust show on your face.

- When the night ends, please do not act like it's a sigh of relief.

I know some partners already do many of these things, but some don't, and it causes problems. As for the day after, it's also important for the husband or wife to thank their spouse. Then, reciprocate at another time with a nice card, dinner, car wash, car detail, spa visit, etc. This is a time for giving and receiving, not give and take!

CRUCIBLE NUMBER TWO: Be respectful at all times

Don't ever make your man feel small, especially in front of another man. Keep him involved during any process, men want to be heard! Refrain from eye-rolling around other men, talking down to him, disregarding him, cutting him off, or asking him questions that you heard another man ask. Keep your emotions in check when at a car dealership and don't allow the car salesman to only talk to you. This goes for any purchase. Don't act like you're the only one that has the "Authority to Buy." When you act this way, exclusion takes place immediately. Keep the husband a part of conversations regarding children. A lot of education officials tend to speak to the mother only. Never argue in public, and if you're in a disrespectful mood, don't do it in front of the kids. When you do that, he loses authority. Once the kids start disobeying him, it's not always about what he doesn't say or do, but more like what you say and do to him around the kids.

Chapter Fourteen

Eye Feel You

Lesson Thirteen: See the love

I learned to listen with my eyes. Eye contact is crucial when communicating. With that, you'll see what lifts her up and what brings her down, either by what you say or do, or what she's saying, during any discussion. A man can learn a lot from a woman when she speaks of her father and a woman can learn a lot when a man speaks of his mother. These are very touching, emotional, and even hurtful times during a conversation. Most times while you're out to dinner, if the conversation gets to this point, the woman will use the restroom a few times. Once to cry and another to look at herself in the mirror to clean herself up (re-do make-up) and then talk to God before she's back in your presence.

"Thank you, Lord—finally, a man that understands me. Whew, yes!"

She puts on more lip gloss and pops her lips!

As a man, you must notice the small, subtle changes in a woman. There are many, but once you let her know you notice a change, it'll let her know how intuitive, instinctive, and thoughtful you are. She'll never tell you what they are, you'll have to notice them for yourself. From the streaks in her hair, a different nail color, a different lipstick or gloss, or a new perfume. The four most important changes or things women want you to notice are:

- Her hair
- Intentional weight loss
- How she looks in a dress
- How her food tastes

Never ask for a woman's age or weight and don't make recommendations unless she asks. Women will hide their tampons, or even try to hide when she's on her cycle. This is a very delicate time for them, and it's delicate in two, maybe three phases.

The first phase is at the beginning of her cycle, which can bring on anger, hot flashes, heightened emotions, crying, pain, and anxiety, depending on how heavy their cycle is. Also, in the first phase, her feelings can be easily hurt, so be very careful with what you say.

The second phase, for some women, is an increase in sex drive, craving food or sweets, and to be held, kissed, or just loved deeply, even for a moment. You first need to identify each phase and during the relationship's talking stages. There may be a time where she'll just go away for a few days. You must remain patient; at this point, it's none of your business. The best you can do is accept her ghostly ways. Don't ever snoop in her bathroom, either. When a woman feels or is bloated, she'll feel unattractive. Compliment and hug her and then give her her favorite treat.

I had to take note of the menstrual cycles of the women that I dated because if you are unaware of it, you can make some detrimental mistakes.

"Aww when we met, your skin was smooth. You got a pimple on your cheek."

Let her think that the acne is covered up with foundation; *don't ever* mention that, *ever*!

Some women don't feel beautiful while on their cycle, so try your best to make her feel that way, regardless of what she's wearing, make-up included.

To make things easier, you need to develop your own cycle alongside hers. Don't ever seclude her because of her cycle.

Eye Feel You is about not only really liking a woman but also about knowing their occasional shift in emotions. It is realizing that there are other beautiful things about her aside from her face and body; they include her intelligence, how she behaves with kids and adults, passion, drive, and integrity. The basic compliments get really old. Come up with some new ones but make sure it's the truth. A lot of women have nice things about themselves but have never been complimented on. For me, I love a woman with a beautiful personality, this supersedes a pretty woman with a horrible personality. I enjoy nice, square foreheads; they just seem sexy to me. A gap in their front teeth, to me, shows confidence, because most women want it closed. Eyeliner brings out a certain sexiness as well. What's really sexy to me is when a woman doesn't wear any make-up. Although I like it when she does, the bare face is just as sexy as one made up by *Mac*! Women who wear suits are very confident and strong. Short hair is the boss, long hair looks nice; just make sure it's well taken care of, either way. Shaved sides are *sexy* as hell, too!

"NATURAL IS NATURE-REAL"

~LEON R. WALKER JR~

Sexy

You like hearing that, don't lie,
I love saying it, that's why.
That's why you like hearing that,
it comes from me, you know me.
That's why it feels good, it's our chemistry.
I choose my words carefully, not to put you down,
but to keep you there for me. There for you,
is where we'll be, to me, that's sexy.
Soul, ecstasy, extra me.
Yes, you see, that's what sexy means to me, SEXY.
It has nothing to do with lying next to me, you see.
Just to be in this world with me, is sex to me.
Why would you be less to me?
I realize that I am blessed to be
in your arms, your breast to me,
feeling your breath is sex to me.
Yes, I get tired, but talking to you is rest to me,
hearing your voice is life to me.
I want you as a wife-to-be, like you see a family holding hands,
is unto thee. Would you be over me,
as I need your protection, when I have fallen down? You see,
that's sexy to me.

Let's Talk- Some of you think because you have a nice car, a nice house, and the kids look and seem happy, everything is ok! Not always the case. Over the years, I've heard plenty of women say "Yeah, we're good." Well, let me tell you, that's not always the case either. A lot of men don't know or get the small things right. I was one of those men.

Asides from the other great qualities that my father had, I probably learned this from him. It's not right on either side, not at all. Some women fail to realize how bad it is to be taken for granted. Most times, if not all, you realize that you are or will be taken for granted, yet you find a way to look past it. You settle, knowing darn well you deserve more and better. Then, either directly or indirectly, you teach your daughters, and in some cases, your own son, to settle.

Your man will, in a shallow way, tell you he doesn't like you by not show-ing you , plain and simple, and you know it. His time around you will subside, his actions will start to become less thoughtful, his words will slowly become one-word sentences; that's when he's starting to fade away. He will reduce the time he spends with the kids. His touch, if he touches you, will be cold and short. You're still sexy but only on the outside, where that's all we see or choose to see.

If he's not connected to God, he's connected to the devil, just like I was. There's no way around it. I know people may not agree with me, but I have lived the life of being a distant lover, all the while knowing nothing about God. I tried to be a patriot, a member of churches, and God, co-opting his ways, thoughts, and even scriptures and making them mine, as resonated with me. You can save him though. Although my parents never spoke of religion in our home, my father was a very moral man.

PEARLS

- Keep her confident around other women.

- If his friends flirt with you, tell him.

- Always be on each other's side.

- When she squirts, give her a cold glass of her favorite juice or wine, and pull the blankets on her.

- Teach her how to taste herself.

- Take her to feed the ducks, and let her sit behind you, on a bench. When she's comfortable, sit behind her.

- Don't feel like she's not into you the first few times you meet. There's a good chance that she used her rabbit before meeting you to keep herself calm.

- Let him vacation with his friends.

- Don't ever over-talk him.

- Don't stare at men or women while you are with your partner.

Chapter Fifteen

Huge Turn-Offs

Lesson Fourteen: No Control is Control

The more you give, the more you get. Give us time and space, and we'll do some of the following: come closer, wonder about you, love you more, and respect you more. We'll also start to see what things we miss about you. Don't smother a man, he'll feel like he's dying and start to miss himself, not you! A lot of women get this part wrong. I do understand that if he was a cheater, you might lose trust and watch his every movement. I was once that guy, so I get it.

If you are afraid to give him room, you won't have any room yourself and the two of you need to talk about growing together (as I delve deep into this, in *Growing and climbing in Love*, and NOT, *falling* in Love), or you'll realize that you are growing apart. Either way, it needs to be discussed because it's obvious. I get it, you eased up and he cheated, maybe again.

Just because you reel him in tighter doesn't mean you've healed him of his addiction to women. He's just not addicted to you and you have to be okay with that, you just might be too much or too strong for a man that isn't ready for your unique, and pure covering. Remember to remind yourself of that beautiful trait. This man will be ok with losing you, and then gaining someone that can't handle him so he knows full well how you're feeling. You're comfortable in being strong and growing, whereas, he's comfortable with someone that's not! His addiction to women could be tied to drugs and her drug addiction. This doesn't mean that there's anything wrong with you; hell, I was quite promiscuous, so your chances of changing me were close to zero. It starts and ends with him—his growth and the possibility of rekindling the relationship.

You might be the type of person whose anger builds and you disrespect him in front of his friends and family. If you won't talk to your son in a certain way, then don't talk to your man that way. You already know it's wrong. Where women make a huge and critical mistake in life and relationships is wanting to or trying to control their man and his money. Your insecurities can be his fault, yes, but if you plan to stay, make sure your plan is to *grow* past his past indiscretions. I know a lot of you don't agree with this. Just remember, you're not a man. I'm speaking from my pain and infidelity. Men cheat recklessly – at least I did. Women tend to be a lot smoother with it.

Just because your mother controlled your father and his money, doesn't mean that you can do that in your relationship. You've seen your dad and how he operates, and you've seen your man's father and how he operates. They're two totally different men. Men watch how you and your mother operate and, in some cases, your mother is much more understanding and likable. Trust me, we see how you treat your sons, how they might run you over yet you still manage to project your pain and anger onto the man. That's not cool.

There are women out there who watch you, just like men watch you and she'll be just fine being the side-piece to get what he refuses to give you, based on how you treat him. You curse at him or even mistreat him but once you see someone else do it, you're upset, because it's wrong. Now is the time for you to adjust how you treat him. A lot of times, when you think your man is sleeping with another woman, he just *might not be*, but I will tell you this: if anything is going on, one of the most *soothing pleasantries* the side piece woman can give a hurting man is a conversation and a listening ear, and through that conversation, he will receive *reassuring confidence!* She can make him strong enough and confident enough to walk away from you, the house, and your kids in an effort to *regain* himself and come back to his kids—not you! This type of man hates being at home and is vulnerable!

Simple women are very attractive—very! This type of woman can drive a man fun-crazy and we adore it. You just need to get up under your pain and find *Her!*

"THE CONTROLLING WOMAN HAS SOME
INSECURITIES THAT SHE HASN'T DEALT
WITH JUST YET. MAYBE SHE'S SEEN HER
MOTHER CONTROLLED BY HER DAD/
STEPDAD, EITHER THROUGH FEAR OR
SOME SORT OF ABUSE—BE IT PHYSI-
CAL, MENTAL, VERBAL, FINANCIAL, OR
SPIRITUAL. SHE THEN VOWS TO NEVER
LET A MAN TREAT HER THAT WAY, BUT
IN THE MEANTIME, SHE LOSES HERSELF
TO A MAN THAT NEVER TAUGHT HER TO
HAVE A HEALTHY RELATIONSHIP WITH
MEN BECAUSE HE NEVER RELATED IN
ANY OTHER WAY APART FROM BEING AN
ABUSIVE DAD OR STEPDAD!"

~ LEON R. WALKER JR~

SHE'S SIMPLE

She's simple, yet those around her don't know.

They're lost in a world she's not lost in.

She's wrong, she's weird, she's crazy,

that's how they thought of her.

Not once has she thought of them that way.

She's simple, yet searching for love, but still sees good in all.

Too simple for simple minds,

yet mindful about simple things, she's simple.

She found that the best love is the love of herself,

a love she lost for years.

She wasted time missing others,

but didn't miss herself enough, or at all.

Simplicity found her, she found simplicity, simply grounded.

I love her forehead, her earlobes, they were forgotten about.

I love her confident walk, her belief in me.

It's all simply natural, natural simply,

I'm simple, she has to be too.

Let's Talk – Not achieving the simplicity of life, the little things that ✝ touch your soul, we go on and on for many years (and for some, forever) looking for happiness but looking in all the wrong places. Those places are beneath the simple things but we look up because we are afraid to look down for the small, simple things. Looking down doesn't mean sorrow, failure, or even being docile. Look down, it's where we started, that's where we'll end up, and that's what we forget.

HER

I want to know her; I don't want to buy her.

She can't be bought or sold, but some men find a way,

some women give themselves away, to be bought and sold.

Some women never find themselves,

they go so deep into rearing children, raising young men,

and in some cases, raising grown men.

Some women never, just never, find themselves.

I want to know her, but I can't.

She doesn't want to know herself,

does she see her mother?

Or does she see at all? When will I know her?

When will she know herself?

Should I buy her and then control her?

I just want US, to know her.

Let's Talk - More often times than not, while working hard to maintain a family or keep people happy, women forget who they are or who they should become. I am not saying maintaining a family is bad, but watching my mother raise us, I saw that she became lost in doing so. All I'm saying is that your life is much more than being a mother and a wife.

Not all women lose themselves, and even for these women, there was a time that they did lose themselves. However, they recovered, but some never do. You live, but you aren't living, just merely existing, and for some, you're ok with that. You stay around long enough to see your kids graduate, go on to college, and now you're left alone. Still married, but alone. Most become comfortable with just dying.

Let me tell you this—it's only the *beginning of your second life*. There is much more happiness either with or without a man, after divorce, or after you've turned fifty and feel like it's over. It's not. I became an author at age fifty, I work out and exercise more now than I did when I was in my twenties, thirties, and forties. I ran my first marathon at age forty-eight, began loving yoga at age fifty-four. I was able to do this by going into my *spiritual being*, following *God's presence* (his presence is constant), reading great articles, and then investing a little time to think about what I read or heard until I saw results.

Most times, the feeling of growth, happiness, and awakening was instant. Was it work? Yes, but not hard work. I wanted worth, more than anything, so I did not consider it work. "What are you worth?" is the magic question you must ask yourself daily. Write it down and literally attack your order. Just like you expect others to follow your orders, follow your own. The body will obey – *it knows what grows*!

It doesn't have to be a physical transformation; for some, it can be mental, or even both. Build up your mental strength in order to walk away from toxic relationships or make yourself strong enough to know and believe that there's nothing wrong with you. I believe that we have three lives to live, two here: from the age of one minute to the age of 120 on earth, living six decades at a time, and the third life with our true and only spirit, once we've done our deeds, here on earth. That's why it's crucial to be nice, understanding, fair, humble, and generous—living in this way, your soul is open to all blessings. Blessings float around us daily, I believe that's God's way of watching over the good-natured people. We are all open to blessings; they hover above us and each time you perform and live as a good-natured soul, there's some sort of deposit into your spirit.

You must believe what you hear in your head, *the positive things*, and know that you're not making these messages up. God—or whomever you believe that entity to be—is talking to you inside, in the depths of your pure soul. Act on it—NOW!

Chapter Sixteen

The Mother/Mommy-Dad

Lesson Fifteen: Can't Let Go

I have discussed different relationship archetypes in previous chapters. Here, we are going to discuss a new one – the Mother-Dad or Mommy-Dad. The Mommy-Dad is a more traditional, old-fashioned type of woman. She's much more well-suited for a man, reared and raised in the South. Mommy-Dads are very caring, loving, and given the nature of women and mothers, she has been chosen to heal and resurrect and also has the power to plant the much-needed seed. The Mother-Dad is a woman that treats her man like she's his father. He'll burn through money, ask for more, and not give a darn. This comes from his being under his mother all the time and not around his father. Mom has bailed him out of jail, depleted her bank account, but keeps hope alive, even in the darkest of moments. His mother knows fully well who her son is and what he's about; she's just happy that he's alive, nothing else really matters. Both he and his mother are okay with this type of upbringing. They have either addressed how he will act once he's in a relationship or totally avoid it. As a young man, he will sometimes think like a woman. In some cases, this is good, but as the man he is supposed to become, this will be fateful in his relationship with a woman, hence—Mother-Dad.

The downside of "Mommy-Dad" is that, depending on what the man chooses to react to: drugs, alcohol, lack of money, transportation, your control over him, he could be quite dangerous. There will be times where he'll miss his father and blame his mother (you, playing the role of his mother) for his dad's absence! At this moment, you'll remind him of his mother in a negative way, not knowing why his dad is gone and no longer around. This could go in any direction: physical abuse, verbal abuse, or death, especially if his mother isn't around to change his manner of thinking. She may not be around because his dad killed her!

Mothers have a hard time letting go and I understand this. They will even overlook his addictions, errors, and weaknesses just to be his crutch and enabler. This happens when a mother becomes lonely and her only saving grace is her grip on her son, regardless of whether it hurts his relationship with his woman or man. He will listen to his mother before he listens to his partner, not because she makes sense but because after she speaks to him, he'll want a favor and she'll grant him one. He'll treat you the same way. Mom will give him good advice but won't discipline or counsel him when he makes mistakes, allowing him to repeat his actions, over and over again. This guy has become so comfortable with lying to his mother and he'll lie to you with ease. He wants to be spoiled and babied and you won't do it because he hasn't earned that treat! He isn't really a Bad Boy, he doesn't have the heart to be rough, but he's conniving, just as sneaky and rotten to the core. Instinctively, you hang in there because you've seen him at his best, hoping that he returns. It's just that the energy and love he puts in other things feel more rewarding to him, so you come third, right after drugs and prostitutes!

A momma's boy, especially when he's grown, knows darn well who he is and how he's acting. He'll resort to his narcissistic ways and even morph into the helpless little boy when he needs to. As the "Mom-Dad", you'll never let go because he's now your investment. You're not accustomed to failure, regardless of how much of yourself you've lost

This man has imprinted himself in your mind and you'll see every other man as a reminder of him the moment they make a mistake, forget to call, or don't keep their word. You become toxic; even with a good heart and mind, you're still damaged, however, not beyond repair. You're a loving person and a giver and that feeds your spirit!

Name-calling is one thing he's good at. *"You're dumb"* is his favorite way of seeing you, leaving at all times of the day and night, lying, etc., but overall, he's heartless. Being a Mother-Dad isn't worth anything; not your life, finances, or health because, with him, all is at stake! You'll believe him when he says to you, *"I'm sorry!"*

GOD DOES NOT CHOOSE THOSE WHO ARE EQUIPPED; HE EQUIPS THOSE HE HAS CHOSEN.

~ANONYMOUS~

I SAID I WAS SORRY

I said it once, you came back, you even let me back in.

I knew what you wanted to hear, so I used that against you.

I knew me, I was honest, but you didn't catch on when I told you,

I was sorry, now I blame you.

I beat you, you held me.

I cheated, you protected me.

you even turned your back on your family for me.

I hid a lot, I even hid, but in your face, I said *I was sorry.*

You love my words, and I knew that,

my words controlled your mind and your world.

You were strong, but you were blind.

Your ears and your heart were in tune,

but your vision didn't go past *me*.

I said I was sorry, and that's all you heard.

That was good enough, and I knew that.

I'm not sorry anymore, I'm a man now,

but you are sick, unhappy, and gone.

I never apologized, *I was sorry*, you know,

pathetic, but you were blind.

I blamed you, then you blame yourself.

Let's Talk - Don't just listen to my words, look at my actions. A lot ✳ of women have their eyes wide shut. Most men know this. Listen to me, don't just hear me, listen to what I am saying to you. Stop being fooled. Pay more attention to your *gut feeling*. That feeling isn't pain, it's emotions. There's a difference; when it's in your gut, your stomach, whatever is in there will affect your thinking and your clarity. It is called a "gut feeling" because it's your *second brain* which deals with emotional shifts!

Also, you need to find out what you're missing. You better do this, because as that type of man, if I find out before you, I'll exploit it every time. You might be educated and highly intelligent, but if I figure out what you're missing, then I have the control, and you'll never know why. I know that what I do manifests in your "gut feeling" and that's why I'll give you gifts, jewelry, and other things you like but never received. I'll feed you, take you to nice restaurants so I can keep your eyes wide shut by controlling your *second brain*! ✳

He says YOU'RE DUMB. And you Ask Yourself, "AM I DUMB?"

"I'm smarter than you."

He looks in your eyes and tells you.

He fails you, on purpose.

You won't know, your intellect won't show.

Your head is down, you're smart enough to know the truth,

but you hide that frown.

You stay unhappy, accept being dumb, he knows where the pain is coming from.

It's too late, you've given up.

It's too late, but you want to sit up,

proud, strong, weak, confused.

You're used, used to it, you let go, let go, let go.

Now she's gone, that wonderful woman won't show, grow.

She's scared to grow, but she won't let go.

"Am I dumb?" I must be, that word fits me, it fits me

because he, he said so, he who doesn't know, me, me, me.

How smart I am, smart enough to stay, stay and prove,

but wait, I don't have to prove, to prove to him that I'm smart.

He's smart, he knows my heart. Another man, a new start,

he's dumb if he gives away my heart, away, away,

I have a way to find me, not dumb you see.

He can't see that another man wants me,

all of me, dumb, *humph*, dumb, *hmph*, no, not me.

I found my courage, I found me, yes, me .

That wonderful woman, so strong, so wise, so happy,

wealthy, a nice size, oh, and oh, I hear his cries.

"Is it true?" I ask him, "is it true, am I smarter than you?"

Let's Talk – Never be okay with being called names. One name is 🦋 too many. There are many names, nice ones that you can be called. A lot of men and women have been and are being verbally abused and they accept it because the perpetrator comes home after with flowers, a nice pair of jeans, shoes, a card, or takes them to dinner a day after calling them names or being bitchy. Name-calling is the beginning of abuse, it will become 🦋 more intense the more you get used to it. After that comes the beating, hospital visits, and hot grease. The abuser doesn't want to lose their grip on you. There are many ways of abuse. Bleaching clothes, cutting tires, keying cars, hitting you then calling the police on YOU. Once they start to lose their grip, you'll end up at the morgue and they'll plead insanity! 🦋

Lesson Sixteen: What You Allow Will Make You Small 🦋

Eventually, you will become so small that the man can make you fit any-where, mostly in his world and not yours!

Women will let a man say anything to them. I've seen this for years and at times, have done so myself. Yes, it was wrong, painful, and hurtful, yet we do it anyway. I don't, anymore.

Lesson Seventeen: Thoughts of a Weak Man/Woman!

"Stay in your place, because once you come out of it, I wouldn't know what to do with you, nor will I know how to handle you."

"You ain't shit, just like yo' daddy, like your mother said."

"Verbal abuse is the only way for me to make you feel like you are less than 🦋 *me. Stay in your place. Remember, you told me your mother was that way, she took care of your father, baby, don't you want to be like your mother?"*

Reverse psychology is used by
✳ people who are afraid of losing
a person; one who has already
lost themselves but can't let you
know that.

~ Leon R. Walker Jr~

PEARLS

- If you are in a relationship, never slow dance with someone else.

- Treat each other's kids the same as you would treat yours. ✶

- Arrive on time—for everything.

- Watch whatever movie she recommends. Stay awake and quiet.

- If she takes a day off, pay her for it.

- Know her shoe size.

- Don't act like a jackrabbit in bed.

- Don't get right up after you have an orgasm. For a woman, this is a very sensitive time for her.

- If you get your man to cum during oral sex, leave him alone for a few minutes for him to enjoy the sensations even more, then start kissing him again.

- Orgasm together. Don't try, do. This works based on the chemistry between you and knowing each other's body language, especially the rhythm.

Chapter Seventeen

I.M.

Lesson Eighteen: *Irresistible Minimum.*

No, this is not spoken about, but for women, the worst part about this is that it can be seen. Your eyes will touch your soul during this process. You're just not aware of it. I developed I.M.! It suited me well.

"Women are emotional; men are physical," they often say. This is a misconception because they leave a major component out—and have left it out for hundreds of years. I suppose no one knew, but I did.

If you believe or choose to separate the physical and emotional states of men and women, as if we're different in that realm, you'll be making your first mistake. From a physical perspective, yes, we're different. However, we all react to stimuli, both negatively and positively. It's all based on what was said, done, learned, thought, experienced, or encountered.

Once you believe this misguidance, which many people have and still do, you divide the inner workings of genetics and DNA. When professionals and authors mention and write about it—writers, doctors, and psychiatrists— they often forget that men are emotional too, sometimes in the same manner as women. Those men have chosen to adopt their mothers' DNA, and that's life changing for them. As men, we are egotistical and because of that, when our ego is damaged, ruptured, challenged, or tested, we become emotional and at that particular moment, we see the woman as responsible for that insult or onslaught!

Your eyes touching your soul, through my I.M.

The *Irresistible Minimum* is the basics that a man has. These are "good-to-haves" and are also easy to attain. So easy that the "Comfort Zone" becomes our goal.

The Irresistible Minimum: A car, well-maintained; a job, doesn't have to be a great job, just as long as I get up every day and go to work; an apartment; a clean bill of health; and a decent credit score. A credit score is something that I'm always willing to discuss. Let's say my score is 680. Now, we'll add my nice conversation skills to all of that. You and I both know that you are already feeling good about me (him), and you can't deny it.

The Irresistible Minimum is shown or discussed from day one. You now see me as your equal, and your plan is to grow from this point on. I see the twinkle in your eyes, your body shifts around, you dance, shake, and roll, but you have no idea—I AIN'T SHIT!

Let this be a valuable lesson for you: all I have to offer is the minimum, and that's all you'll get from me, but you like my minimum. I know and maintain just enough to keep my hooks in you and you have no idea that I'm a minimalist! You'll remain faithful, but I won't. I can't be, the numbers are just too high to resist. I become more and more promiscuous with every woman I meet.

I was always happy with and around women. Being from Cleveland, Ohio, military men were rarely seen, so being one meant you were a hot commodity in my town. The ratio of women to men in many cities can range from five to one, all the way up to twelve to one, or more. One thing is for sure, I was greedy, gritty, and nasty as a single sinner could be. With these numbers, why would I settle down with you? I had every kind to choose from. Short hair, long hair, nappy hair, hood rat, side piece, thick, skinny, welfare (these are fun and dangerous and really easy to like), dark, light, redbone, big lips, wide mouth, tall, short, weird, crazy, all of that, and I had it all. Don't even talk about marriage.

What's really sad about this is that women will become role players because they'd rather have a piece of a man, as opposed to having the whole, entire, cheater. This means they can be much less emotionally invested. They know the numbers are in the man's favor, too.

You will be faithful to a player because he's nice-looking, pays attention to you, takes you on nice— and I mean really nice—dates, gets your hair and nails done, massages you, communicates well, plays with your kids, gives you great advice. He shows up late, but when he does, he'll have a treat because he listens to what you like. I often showed up late on purpose, bearing gifts because I knew that your anger and happiness would make you conflicted inside. I smelled good and you liked my smile, so you couldn't stay mad for too long.

Twenty-six-year-old Leon:

"Why are you late, Leon?"

"I had to drop ol' girl off. You know the one I told you was a little crazy?"

She huffs and puffs and looks away, out the passenger side window.

"Damn baby, you look sexy and delicious. I like your neck, can I lick it?"

I leaned over and licked her neck, not a kiss. I licked it. Her shoulders went up, slowly.

"I told you about her, remember?"

"Yeah, but...damn...oooooooo...I can't stand you!"

"Yes, you can. Now gimme a kiss, I love your lips. Here's a small gift. Here, I got you some of my favorite lip gloss, put it on and let me lick it off."

"Okay."

I make small talk to check her "temp in regards to erature."

"Remember, ol' girl. She's cool but I cut our date short. Broke my neck, to get here to be with you."

She now speaks in a slow, soft voice.

"Yeah, I remember her. Can I have another kiss, please?"

After feeding the ducks at Forest Hills Park, we spend the night in downtown Cleveland in the flats. We are sitting in my car, on the banks of the lake, listening to the waves and The Isley Brothers and talking. I wake up to breakfast the next morning.

This was my routine, my minimum but her maximum exposure to being treated like a lady. Planning a night on the town is a major part of the Irresistible Minimum. Women like and enjoy a spontaneous man, one that thinks differently than most men, and although I was a player, I was honest about taking advantage of the ratio.

✳ I do not recommend that young men do and act the way I did. It's physically and mentally unhealthy and disrespectful, to say the least. Women deserve better. If you don't want your sister or mother to be played, then don't be a player. Like I said about my dad, he wasn't a player even though many women loved him. He wasn't promiscuous like I was. I developed this distasteful quality and spread myself thin, all over the world.

I can tell you exactly when it all started. I didn't have to go the route that I went to, but I did! I almost lost my life, and from the hurt, I, like many other abused women, vowed to never, ever, let this happen to me again. However, in my case, I was the abuser, verbally, and emotionally abusing and neglecting my ex, so I had no choice, but to accept any karma coming my way!

I would like to take you on a quick journey, for a moment, concerning my truth. I retrieved three chapters from my upcoming book, *One Point*, that I feel are extremely relevant to *Loveship* in an effort to extend an invaluable and inside look into a once happy, respectful kid who turned into an unhealthy, toxic Sailor.

Now, so that you can gain a clear and concise inside look, into a young, arrogant, and emotionally detached monster, I present to you all, the young man with a promising career who was quickly headed for a Bad Conduct Discharge from the United States Navy. I feel it is essential for young men and women alike to read, learn, and digest, but mainly to understand many more things about someone that's just like them.

First, your words will hurt and cut people deep to the core, so choose your words carefully and wisely. Secondly, once you convey your feelings, good or bad, true or not—in my case, despicably spoken—prepare for what could possibly happen next. In these next chapters, you will witness my immaturity along with my demons and my turning point, when my promiscuity and lack of respect for women reared its ugly head. My life takes a drastic turn, one that hit so deep and hard in my heart and soul, that I didn't want to be on this earth anymore! Only by the grace of God am I still alive to tell this story! ✷

Chapter Eighteen

Shattered Heart

"If you want to discover a new *you*, a different *you*, a great *you*, tell yourself positive things. If you want to discover a *you* that's toxic, dangerous, mean, and nasty, tell someone hurtful things. Both will happen, it's your choice!"

I *do not* recommend the latter; I lived through it to tell my story! Hateful, nasty, evil people are asking for help and they don't even know it. We are too busy and more consumed with making other people feel sad or hurt, just to mask or hide our own pain. By embodying those traits and affecting other people, without caring, I was already toxic in many ways. My childhood pain and wicked ways really started to take hold of me the older I got. I never asked for help, I thought I had it all together, but it had already fallen apart, many years ago. I never picked up the pieces; instead, I stepped on them, killing the little boy that was always crying out for help: *Diablo is back!*

February 1991, San Diego, California

"I don't like you, I don't love you, and I will sleep with every woman possible, while I'm overseas."

In retrospect, these words changed my life for the better (as it set me on a path that taught me a lesson), but the worst came first!

The night before, I had laid in the bed, looking at the ceiling fan going round and round. She was lying next to me, wanting to cuddle. I was cold-minded and cold-hearted, distant. My mind was focused on the women overseas, Asian, Puerto Rican, Indian, you name it. There was already a festival going on in my head, and I had to be a part of it. I had already imagined my success as a sexual deviant, long before it even happened, so I was destined to wake up not wanting to be with her. The manifestation consumed my mind and body throughout the night, then settled in.

I uttered those nasty words, to my girlfriend the morning before we deployed.

It was 0630 am in San Diego, California. A bit chilly outside because it was February. The sun had come up, my suitcase was packed; I had condoms on the zipper side. I peeped out the window to see if my ride was there. I didn't want her to take me to the pier to see me off because I was already disconnected from her but she had no clue, yet I was!

It was time for a three-month deployment. A very short cruise onboard a reserve Fast Frigate. In our household, we never heard the word "love." It wasn't mentioned between my parents, it wasn't said anywhere in my family, nor was it said amongst my siblings and me. We just, kind of, in a way, knew that we had love for each other. After all, my siblings and I had to bond in such a way that the care and feeling of love were there, but we never said it. This will hurt you as a man or woman when in a relationship if it's not something that you are accustomed to saying, hearing, or are familiar with. Without the knowledge of love or the familiarity of professing it, you are at a loss as to how to convey it. You may not even feel it. I didn't! *Lust* resonated deep in my spirit!

This thought process is prevalent, especially in a man or woman who knows love and

either want to hear or need to hear it. In my case and in my relationship at that time, she needed to hear it but I could not deliver. She missed her father and I could not replace him. After all that I had gone through, all that I had put myself through, my only saving grace was my looks, physique, and conversational skills; most times that wasn't enough, mainly because my conversations were based on sex and nothing of substance. I got away with it for years. For a long time, this was what carried me through relationships and helped me get women; this was what I thrived on. I was missing the components of a healthy relationship my entire life. They would only come to me when I turned fifty years old! Just in time to teach my kids. I was a wreck; the devil was looking over me but God was watching over him. The devil was once an angel and so was I. *Not anymore!*

"When I get back, I'm done, with you!"

"Leon don't, please don't. Why are you saying these mean things to me? Why?"

"I just don't want to be with you anymore. I don't love you, Terry! I hope you are gone when I get back in three months. Take all of this crap, I don't care, you can have them."

Terry cried and I stood there watching the pain course through her body. I was motionless and heartless. She pulled the covers over her head and continued to cry. It sounded horrible but I quickly deflected any remorse.

"What the hell you crying for, it's just a relationship, *damn*! I'm out. Bye, go to hell, Terry!"

My ride pulls up and we head to the pier at 32nd Street, Naval Base San Diego.

"Dog, you look pissed, man, you alright?" My friend asked.

"Naw man. Terry in there cryin'. I don't want to hear it, man!

I adjust my seat and put my seatbelt on. "Let's go, man."

From the driver's seat, Larry looks at me with concern in his eyes. He's a real grown man and knows about the path I am about to go on—he's been down it before—but I don't listen to his counsel.

"Okay man, you sure? We gonna be gone for three months, man. You don't want to go back in there and make-up?"

"Nah, I'm good, she'll be here when I get back, watch!"

"Man, you better stop mistreating that woman, man."

"Larry, stay out my business, man She good, she ain't goin nowhere, ya know!"

"Okay, Walker, I'm here for you. I am."

"Man, you act like I don't do anything for her. I buy her clothes, take her out, we drink, party, you know, stuff like that. I mean, what else do I have to do, she all mushy, wantin' to hold hands and caress, I ain't down with that man!"

"You need to start doing other things too. Those are important to women and they want time too. Do you talk to her?"

I pause, put my hand on my chin, sit back, and think.

"Naw, I don't do all that mushy stuff, nope. She knows I don't like that, so we good, Larry, we good."

"Okay. As I said, I'm here for you, Walker. I'm only telling you this because I've been through it. I got hurt before man, it's painful, and I don't want to see you go through any hurt or pain, ya know."

"Man, my mother left me. Ain't no more hurt in this world like that, so I'm good!"

Most men would call back home when we'd pull into port. Not me. I looked for the bars, clubs and the women. I was having a ball. Little did I know that my soul was being prepared to be opened, cleansed, and replaced, and it would hurt worse than when my mother left me, after all.

March, 1991.

For about one month after leaving home, I still hadn't called home. I didn't even care until I started drinking. A few friends and I were always hitting the clubs, dancing, drinking, and flirting, looking for the next victim or "straggler" as we liked to call them. Stragglers were those women left at the end of the night, sitting at their tables, along with their heads hanging down, just praying someone would come to take them away, but no one wanted them. Sailors said they were either too big, not good-looking enough, or sloppy drunk. I never referred to them as too big, though. Either way, they were the easiest choice. If you spent too much time on the nice ones and didn't get anywhere, stragglers were it. Just like chicken-heads back home, jump-offs, or side pieces, they were plentiful overseas. They even had Asian chicken heads! I thought that term used was very disrespectful as well.

Usually, when ships deploy, some Sailors do not call home right away. They take some time off and that's precisely what I did. Why would I call home? After all, I had broken up with my girlfriend that morning in February 1991. The difference between the other guys and me was that I left on bad terms. Never do that before deploying. It'll be your worst mistake.

We hit the clubs, danced and drank all night and then headed back to the ship. While deployed, we were out to sea with the USS Acadia, a submarine tender on which my sister was deployed. It had lots of women on board. We pulled into Hong Kong right before my sister's ship so I wasn't able to see my sister, but we did communicate via flashing light which was pretty cool. Liberty call went out. A group of us got together and decided to buy some nice outfits and then go to Kowloon to get some silk ties. I just knew that my tie was the best-looking. We hit a club downtown called Crossroads; a cool place with great music, but what was even better was that I saw this beautiful woman. She was the bartender. Her skin was like caramel color, she had lovely, flowing hair and a beautiful face to go with it. Besides all of that, she had a great personality. She could handle all of the trash-talking Sailors at the bar trying to get drinks *and* her. We'll call her Razi.

Razi was brilliant and beyond smart, which made her even more attractive. We ordered our drinks at the bar. We were all dressed pretty nice, and for some reason, I think this caught her eye.

"Razi, hey, who has the best tie in here tonight? Do you mind voting on it for us?" My friend would ask.

Now, being from Cleveland, I had a pretty good eye for clothes. I learned this from the older guys in our neighborhood and my sisters' male friends down in the Hough, Wade Park area who took pride in dressing sharp. Razi decides to join in and votes on the best tie. I just knew that my tie would win. But alas...

"Oh no, your tie is terribly ugly," she said.

I was shocked, drunk, and pissed.

"*What*? Go to hell, you don't know what you talkin' about." I walk away, mad.

We all danced that night, drank, ordered chicken, and flirted with the girls but I was hooked on this beautiful, sexy bartender with the most beautiful lips and a wonderful accent. Razi was very engaged with the crowd, music, and doing her thing behind the bar as well. She didn't miss a beat that night. She knew a lot about many worldly things and about America, specifically the Masons, which caught me by surprise. She had visited our biggest cities, was well-versed about our president, the Ku Klux Klan, and a host of other things.

We had many conversations that night and even though she didn't like my tie and I had said some mean things to her, we still wound up hanging out later that night and the remaining time in Hong Kong. I had just met her and she was younger than I was but we connected on a level that I had never connected with a woman in my life. Our conversations were serious and the chemistry felt good. However, in the back of my mind, I was thinking, Am I over my ex-girlfriend? Is this chemistry real or am I just filling a void? I actually thought a lot about those things but being with Razi felt so good, so real, it couldn't be wrong. In a way, after meeting her, I let go of all of my negative thoughts from my breakup. She made me feel whole again even though my ex-hadn't done anything wrong. Razi had moved me in such a way that it felt like a very close relationship, and it was. Maybe I was searching for something, looking to connect in a way other than a sexual way, and with Razi, I had that. It was amazing.

April 1991. Sasebo, Japan.

We pull in, hit the club, and enjoy the festivities. Japan was a blast. To me, the funny thing was that Japanese people liked American food, music, and men. Black, White, Puerto Rican, Mexican, it didn't matter. The women in Japan are very cool. They can dance, sing, and are generally very talented. The hood clubs were the best. I was surprised to hear lots of rap music, Luther Vandross, Al Green, and Barry White. We even had ribs, chicken, rice and gravy, neck bones, greens, cornbread; it seemed like their menu was made for African-Americans. They had it all.

We head out again. On our way from the restaurant and back to the club, I see some phones outside. We're about a month away from returning home back to San Diego. We had been gone for two months and I was a hot mess once again. We leave the club at about 5:00 am in the morning. My friend decides to call his woman back home in San Diego.

"Yo Walk, are you calling home man?"

"Nah, for what man? Me and my girl broke up."

"Yeah right, you all have been together for a while man. Go ahead and call home, everything will be okay."

He had no clue what I had said to Terry when I left back in February. In my cocky, arrogant mind, I'm thinking "yeah, he's right. There's no way we are through." In fact, up until this point, a woman had never left me. I always initiated the breaking up. I thought it would never happen to me.

I get to the phones outside the club and pull out my calling card. It's 5:00 am in the morning when I make that call. Before calling, I had a horrible gut feeling. Even though I was drunk, a feeling came over me that something was drastically wrong. Calling home two months after a break up is one thing but calling home when you're drunk is an utterly sobering experience. I dialed those dreadful numbers. I'm shaking because I know this call isn't going to go well, not at all. Not to mention, the words that came off of my tongue that day when I was leaving San Diego were still in the air. I knew those words were still in her heart. "I don't love you" were the words that I uttered and I said them with such confidence, arrogance, and without any reservation.

I'm trembling now, my hands are shaking, my palms are sweating. It's dark outside the club. I look up to see that dawn is upon us. The wind is blowing so I kneel down so that when she does answer, I can hear her clearly, after all, I was drunk and very emotional. The whole time, the phone was pressed against my ear, and my nose was running. I'm sniffing but not crying. I remembered what I had said to her. In a way, I was already expecting the worst, but as I said, no woman had ever left me, so my arrogance had come back to me while my fingers were pressing those numbers on the phone. I am just a tad bit confident as I begin to dial her number. As I finish (mind you, it was our home number), I take a deep breath and look around at my friends. They're all smiling with their faces buried in the phones, happy and laughing. In the background, I could hear them say, "Okay baby, I love you too." It would have been nice to end my phone call with those words. But I had left San Diego saying "I don't love you!"

The phone rings and my heart beats fast. I knew what I said was wrong.

"Hello?"

"Hi Terry, how are you?"

"Leon."

"Yes, how are you, Terry?"

In a shallow, sensual voice, Terry brought my world crashing down.

"I can't talk, Leon, I have company. He's here, lying next to me." Dial tone.

I was always told that the only thing open after 2:00am, are legs!

She had to rush off the phone. She wasn't mine anymore. She was gone. My words had hurt her so badly that she had sought comfort from another man. I was crushed. I fell to my knees and that was the first time I had cried since I was a little kid when my father had come to move out of our house. I hadn't cried that hard in 12 years. It seemed like all of the pain from my upbringing gushed out of my soul with just those six words,

I can't talk, I have company.

One word can change a person's life, but six can change a man's entire being, heart, mind, body, and soul. I was devastated and on my way into a black hole, a downward spiral that would last for years. The memories actually lasted forever, the pain lasted for years, but that moment seemed like it lasted for a lifetime. It closed my heart, shattered my soul and crushed my ego, and I had commitment issues for years all because of my words and by no fault of hers.

The feeling made my body numb; it felt like my heart was made of glass and had just been broken into a million pieces, pieces that filled and sliced my veins, the blood escaping through my pores. I literally died on the inside from that phone call. My brain and mind immediately reverted to when my mother left us when my father left our home and, as wrong as I was for maltreating her, I felt like Terry had abandoned me too.

If you were abused, abandoned, or dealt with anything negative in childhood and you do not get or seek help, you will surely have insecurities when you grow older, man or woman. You'll become someone who casts blame onto others, refusing to take the blame for your own indiscretions, and enabling will become your crutch. Many of your relationships will suffer in some form or fashion. You'll engage in self-medication, mutilation, your health will deteriorate, and your mental state will erode. This, of course, will happen over some time, but any type of development will stagnate. This can also be passed down to your kids!

PEARLS

- White women don't like to be called "cunts" and black women don't like to be called "bitches."

- When she tries to get out of bed, grab her, pull her close and whisper, "Just a few more minutes, baby!"

- Buy him nice razors, socks, T-shirts, and underwear. Never buy cheap stuff from the dollar store!

- Don't get with your mother and plan with her on a project for your husband to do. When you do this, it seems like your mom is running the house. Some men will start to pull back. You will then start to slowly lose him.

- Ladies, practice with a cucumber and not a banana, as the banana will give in, and even break, giving you a false sense of your grip and intensity.

- If you want to learn how to perform oral sex really well on your woman, speak with a gay woman, in great detail. Don't tell her who your woman is though.

- Do you and make him miss you. It's not about torture but give a little at a time, not all at once.

- Leave your husband completely alone 1-2 days a week. His love for and attraction to you will grow.

- Never lust for your ex.

- Don't smother your partner.

Chapter Nineteen

Night Stalker

"Yo, *Esse, lemme get* a bottle of Cisco!"

We pulled into San Diego in May of 1991 and Terry isn't on the pier. All of the other guys' families and wives are on the pier, but not Terry. Three hours after our return to our homeport, Terry came to see me, very late. She wasn't the same woman I had left months earlier. She even looked different and seemed happy and in charge. And indeed, she was. I was at her mercy and there wasn't anything that I could do about it. The tables had turned!

"What's up, Terry, you look nice!"

"Leon, stop. It's too late. I'm gone. Your compliments don't mean shit to me anymore. I tried to warn you. I told you I was vulnerable."

"Can we just talk for a moment? How 'bout we get a room and chill? I have plenty of money."

"Lemme call my girl and let her know where I am. You don't look right, Leon. I'm scared!"

"Huh, call yo girl? Whatchu mean, I don't look, right? You scared, what?"

"Look, we gon' do this or not? If we do, you payin'."

"Okay, I'll pay. Let's go."

I had sex on my mind, she didn't. Terry had her confidence back and I had lost mine!

She saw the monster in my eyes well before I did. She was right, mentally and I wasn't!

We go to the hotel and after an hour or so, we lay in the bed, just like we were when I cursed her out and left her hurting in our apartment.

"Can we cuddle, Terry?"

"Nah, I'm good——" She's looking up at the ceiling fan, going round and round.

"I need to call my girl. Leon, I'm different, it's just not the same!"

Terry picks up the hotel room phone.

"Girl, I ain't doin' nothing. He's laying right here, lookin' all sad and shit!"

"Who is that? Who are you talking to?"

"None of your business. They helped me when I was hurting and you weren't there for me. They looked out for me, so don't worry about it!"

Usually, I would *snap*, go off. But not today.

"Ok, I'm sorry. Terry, can you hold me?"

"Leon, for you, I'm empty. There's nothing there. He fills me up!"

"He? Who?"

"I'm not telling you his name...you know what? His name is Ellis. He's a Marine, Leon!"

"You...you...you have a boyfriend, Terry"?

"No, I have a man."

My eyes open wide, I lose my breath and my knees buckle beneath me. I start crying. Being on the other side of hurt, the other side of not being wanted, pierced my soul, deeply. I couldn't handle it.

That day, we didn't kiss or anything, and we were always kissing. She was always chewing on my lips, grabbing my face, touching me, rubbing me, always all over me. Not anymore. I was just there and so was she. I began to want her again but she could not stand the sight of me. I had bought food, thinking we were going to have a nice dinner in the room. I bought flowers and paid for the room, of course, but got nothing in return. Not that I deserved anything. Even if she hadn't told me that she had a man, I knew. Her skin was glowing, her hair was short and sexy, her lips were glossed up, her perfume smelled wonderful, but it wasn't for me. The time we spent in the room was horrible and rightfully so. Terry was no longer mine and I could not believe it. I couldn't take it in. I refused to believe that she was gone.

Good girl gone bad and good again. Good because she had a man that gave her everything that I didn't. He did the simple things; Ellis held her hand, he told her nice things, and whispered in her ear, he put her on a pedestal. He put her before his friends, I never did that, didn't know how to.

"I have to go. Ellis is waiting on me."

"Terry, just tell me you are leaving, please don't tell me why and for who you are leaving. I can't take hearing that."

"Leon, you need to hear this. You don't have a choice. You didn't give me a choice!"

She dropped me off back on base and left me standing right there on the pier. I was done. Now, I wanted her to come to the pier; I didn't want that when we left, back in February.

Watch your words.

After two months of struggling to get myself together, I didn't get a haircut, didn't shave, went to work late, stopped working out, and stayed on the ship the entire time. I had just given up. Terry would not take my phone calls; she wouldn't see me. She was always going up to where the Marines were. She damn near moved in with him. It hurt badly. After about a month of trying to get her back, I decided to try and step it up, I legitimately lost my mind!

I finally leave the ship after almost two months of being a hermit, a recluse. I head to our old apartment, the one Terry and I had in San Diego. I looked bad; no haircut, no shave. I had even lost weight. I was down from 190 pounds to 165!

"Greg, can you give me a ride to my old apartment, man?"

"Yeah, sure can. Hop in."

Greg and I get to our apartment and park out front. He has no idea that my stalking has just begun.

"Just sit here for a minute, man. I'm waiting on old girl to come out. When she does, just follow her, I'm meeting her for lunch, cool?"

"Yeah man, all good. Walker, you look bad man, *damn!* What's going on? You good, fool?"

"Oh, nothing. I'm good. I'm good, man. Just meeting my girl for lunch."

"Man, you need a haircut, you need to shave, and you *need to eat.*"

"I know. We're doing all of that today. Thanks for the ride, I'll holla at you later."

Greg knew something was wrong with me but he had no idea what I was going through, nor did he know he'd just dropped me off, *at her job!* I now knew where she worked.

I jog down the street to catch a quick sale at the pawnshop.

"Hi, sir. How much for that right there?"

"Uhh, that will be $450.00. You want it? A special day coming up, huh? Get'n married?"

"Yeah, yeah, I am. I'm about to propose to my girl, she works down the street. Is there a flower shop nearby?"

"Yeah, sure. Right there." He points across the street.

I pay $450.00 for an engagement ring at the pawnshop and jog quickly across the street to buy a dozen roses and some chocolate. I walk to Terry's job, walk up the stairs, and wait in the lobby for what seemed like forever. I was a nervous wreck!

"Hi, Ma'am, I'm Leon. Is Terry here?"

"Ohhhhh, I've heard about you. What are you doing here? You can't see her."

"Yea, ok. Try and stop me and see what happens."

"Sir—sir, don't go back there, you don't have permission. I'll call the police on you."

I head to the back office, flowers in hand, ring in the other hand. I see Terry and don't waste any time.

"Terry, I need you. I'm sorry about what I said, I didn't mean it. Can you take me back?"

"Leon! No! You have to leave, now! Look, this is Ellis."

She slowly swings her arm across her desk, displaying Mr. Ellis, pausing at each picture. I'm sick to my stomach! Terry sits at her desk, her right hand under her chin like she's Bob Barker showing all the gifts on stage. She smiles and her face lights up. I didn't want to, but I just had to look at his pictures. I had to. He took my girl away from me. I gave her to him.

Visions of them having sex shoot through my mind, constantly, rapidly. I lose control.

I drop to one knee, still holding the flowers and extending the ring. "Terry, will you marry me?"

"Leon, get out of here, no…. no way."

"Terry, please, will you…" The receptionist walks in.

"Sir, let's go. You have to leave."

The police and the front desk lady escort me out.

Chapter Twenty

You Ain't Leavin' Me!

I head back to the ship, go to sleep, and start my painful routine all over again. Cry in the morning, cry at lunch, call her, she hangs up. I cry at night, then go to bed. The only way for me to stop the pain was to drink myself to sleep. There was a liquor store on the corner in downtown San Diego that I would frequent. My drinks of choice: St. Ides, Cisco, and a forty ounce of old English malt liquor beer! Drinking had become a daily routine for me.

For days, weeks, I had become a stalker and a drunk. Terry had no clue. I could not accept the fact that she was gone. Somebody had to tell me something. She moved out of our old place and was now with one of the few friends we both knew. It wouldn't take me long to find her, either. I was now catching the bus to get to her location.

"Yo, *Esse* can I have a bottle of Cisco and a 40oz of Old English?"

Mixing the liquor made me *SUPER CONFIDENT!* I'd clench my jaws and get to movin'!

It's about 11:00 pm. I get off the bus on C street and walk to Terry's friend's apartment. There's a tall, black, iron gate that had to be about fifteen feet high. I stand there, look it up and down, and grab the knob. It's locked. I shake it a few times but that does nothing.

"How do I get in here?" I say to myself out loud.

I wait for a few minutes. I wasn't going to just sit there and slowly drink the Cisco and Old English; I had a gate to climb. So once the Cisco got low, I poured the rest in with the 40oz of Old English and chugged them both down. It actually tasted pretty good. Within 15 minutes, I was numb and dazed. My mind went dark and I'm crying. *C'mon, man, get it together!*

At this time, I was talking to myself quite often, and answering, too. The stalking had taken over! Setting the empty bottles down, they clank on the cement sidewalk. I look to my left and right, trying to figure out a way to get beyond this gate. I walk around the entire building. Being downtown, you could easily get shot at that time of the night, especially in that neighborhood which was dominated by the Crips, and I was looking suspicious. After ten to fifteen minutes, I decided to make my way beyond the tall gate. I jump up, get a nice grip on the small poles, whip my feet up onto the other poles, pull myself up, and scale down the other side.

She's staying at apartment B. I stand there looking up the cement stairs. I cringe at the sight of candlelight flickering in the window. My mind instantly starts to imagine Terry and her man being romantic. My heart beats faster. I can feel the anger and fear boil up inside me. I could hear my teeth grinding! I had no clue who was in there.

"*Whelp* here goes. I'm knocking on that damn door," still talking to myself out loud. I try to peep through the window; this is a very dangerous thing to do in any neighborhood. I'm just asking to get shot. I can't see anything through the thick curtains apart from the flickering candles. I tap on the door, no answer. I tap again, no response. Then I begin to knock, and each time no one answers, I knock harder.

"Who is it?" A woman's voice pierces through the door.

"Yo, yo, yo, Sheila, where's Terry?"

"Wait, let me open the door."

"Sup, girl? How you been?" I give Sheila a hug.

"I'm good, Leon. She's not here. Leon, I'm about to leave. We're headed to the club. You good? You been drinking, boy? Whew you stink! Look atcho eyes!"

"Ok, cool, yeah, I'm cool. I have to take a piss, drank a little, you know. Can I u...u...use...the bathroom?" Now I'm completely drunk!

"Sure. My ride is outside, close the door when you leave."

I was buzzed pretty tough but confident as hell. Sheila was really cool. Off and on, she'd try to give me intel about Terry. She and Terry weren't really cool. Since she met Terry through me, she was on my team. Leaving me in their apartment by myself wasn't a good idea. I had Terry's room all to myself.

The first thing I do is look into her panty drawer for anything out of the ordinary. We did have a healthy sex life, so I knew what she liked. I didn't find anything extra, but I did see all sorts of pretty, new panties. Different styles, styles she'd never worn with or for me. There was nothing in that room that was about me. Why would there be?

I had to find a way to reconnect myself with Terry. I continue to look through her brown wooden drawer, full of panties. I pause every few seconds and drop my head then lift it back up again. The pain is overwhelming. I stand in front of her mirror. The candles kept flickering; it felt so sensual, so romantic, but I was alone. I gather myself and allow my feelings to flow. Looking in the mirror, I watched myself sniff her panties, all of them, one by one!

July 1991, Friday morning, 3:00 am.

The days and weeks go by. Terry moves and I find her new place, each time. I didn't dare to go out because I didn't want to see her in the club with her boyfriend, so each weekend, from May to July, I'd sit on her stairs until she'd come home, just to talk to her. I'd sit there for six, seven, even eight hours, sometimes throughout the night, just hoping to see her. Most weekends she wouldn't even come home. This drove me nuts! There were a few times when I'd see a car come close, slow down, then drive on. It was probably Terry and her man, seeing me sitting on her porch and just keep going. I had to stop sitting in the open and the only way I could do it was by hiding, away from the porch.

Saturday morning, 03:00 am. A burgundy car pulls up and I hear laughter. I sit back, waiting. Terry and I were mutual friends with a cool white lady who liked black guys. I didn't know they were hanging out but anytime she'd hang with Rochelle (who was married), I knew they were either with men or chasing men. I had come to hate her. The car rolls in front of the apartment, slows down, stops, and then they proceed to come up the driveway. They didn't see me sitting on the stairs because I was buried in the bushes, it was around 3:00 am.

"Girl, I had a great time, thank you!" Terry gets out of the car, stumbling.

I hop out of the bushes "Terry, where you been?"

"Leon? None of your business," Rochelle says with a snappy attitude. "She doesn't like you, so you need to leave her alone."

"Mind yo' business, Rochelle, I'm not right, right now. Don't talk to me, *bi*..."

"*Rochelle, Rochelle*, just leave him alone, please! Leon, don't call her names!

"Get yo' girl, Terry."

I walk up to the driver's side door, biting my bottom lip. Rochelle and I go back and forth, and I eventually walk away. Terry goes into the house and locks the door. I sit there until 8:00 am that morning; she never goes out. By noon, I wake up, still on the cement stairs. I get up and catch the bus back to the base.

It had been two months of me trying to get Terry back. Two months of climbing fences and hiding in bushes but nothing worked. I'd call her daily, hourly. I even called her mother hundreds of times, nothing worked. I sucked at my Navy job. I could not concentrate, I wasn't working out, eating, and was crying daily. At this point, I was down to 155 pounds from a solid 190 pounds, had bags under my eyes, and was a mess. Most days, I didn't even brush my teeth or shower or change clothes. I felt better when I was dirty while stalking.

I was broken down into my most fundamental form; a great time to start over and rebuild my morals for a healthy relationship. However, I went the opposite route. This was my time to thank God and be a man, instead, I intentionally opened my soul and my mind to Satan. I wanted revenge, so I asked Satan to help me, and he sure did!

"What is Love? Please help me find it, Lord!"

If you believe in the wrong person, men and women will stalk when hurt. Satan put me on a road that felt so good, but it was also so evil!

Lessons will come back to you in many ways. For me, it was through *stalking*. All lessons are *life-altering*, and if you hurt someone, they should alter not only your life but also your way of thinking and how you treat people. So, you must take heed. Regardless of how you receive your lesson, ensure that you have learned from it, in an effort to grow. Some people never do, and they either continue trekking down a downward spiral that may include hurting their partner, kids, career, or even death.

I didn't stalk her to hurt her, I did it because I wanted answers, I wanted her to save me. I wanted to close my wounds as soon as they opened and take my heart back, to gather myself but I gave it away, along with my blessings when I ventured into my *soul ties*. Now, it was, unknowingly, my duty to endure the pain of my wicked ways and the hurt that I subjected her to. Although I was intricately involved with the devil, even he couldn't bring me back!

There wasn't anything that I could have done at that time, and if you cheat, be prepared to take the same journey that I took. It will not be under your control either, *trust me*!

In addition to being in utter disbelief that a woman could possibly leave me, regardless of what I said to her, I had also become a shell of a man— and this was only the beginning. I wasn't deserving to know why and how she moved on because I pushed her into the arms of another man. Now, he had what I neglected, I just had to accept that.

I was always the one leaving a relationship. It hurt like hell to do so, and when my mother left me as a child, I thought that there was no greater pain—but there was.

In my other relationships, I left on my terms, but with questions left unanswered—both in my heart or hers. It is dangerous and I highly recommend that you think it over before you depart. If you do depart, I ask that you conduct a deep soul search to see if you have suffered from abandonment as a child, or at any time during your life and relationships.

If so, your need to leave and your inability to remain in a relationship and work it out is rooted in something that has been done to you by someone else or something that happened to you. It's not your partner's fault. If you continue this way, you could be losing someone that you need in your life, for many reasons. That person could possibly heal you, or at least, help you to get on the right path. They're not there to continue the hurt or watch you hurt yourself. Just stop for a moment and resist the stubbornness!

Back to Terry. Naturally, she and I had a connection and when you discon-
nect, as I did—without notice or fair warning—all of the energy—whether
good or bad—leaves with the relationship. What remains is positivity, for
her. She'll hurt but she'll come out of the hurt much quicker than the man
or the perpetrator. A faithful woman, one that knows God can and will
cover her man. I lost that covering so my soul, *as rotten as it was*, had to
be dealt the wrath.

For a woman looking to get married, become a wife, and have a good life,
she was doing right by *investing in the relationship*, unlike myself. She
will possess her own residual energies—positive ones—simply because
she was honest, genuine, and *in it*. I wasn't. This is why women recover
quicker than men when the man leaves. For me, I received the negative
energy residuals and since I left her with exertion, she had the ability to
move forward. When you do that, you give her the ability to recuperate
and you're then left with inertia. This is when the begging, crying, and
pleading begins. You will be left helpless and there is but one thing to do
at that moment. Let go of your pain and hers, because you created it, and
begin your journey of growing. I felt like I developed a chemical imbal-
ance with no end in sight. Not only did I want answers, but I also wanted
her to let me know that it will be okay, but she didn't! She made 'our' ok,
his soiree!

Men leave, then mourn; women mourn, then leave. As a man, I only had
an entry plan, to enter her body, soul, spirit, and mind, so I wasn't ready
for the exit when all those were gone!

Because I was a good-natured kid, at one time, I wasn't lucky. I was being
watched and guided, therefore I am still alive to tell you about my les-
sons. Women will hold on to the last minute of a broken relationship, and
in most cases, they think of us long after we're gone, because we're not
totally gone and that's the beginning stages of stalking. As men, once
the fear sets in, of either losing her, or ourselves, we take flight, both

mentally and physically--physical flight mindset takes over first. We look for someone to fill the void of the coldness that we feel from our partner that we're currently neglecting. The woman is equipped to leave, she does this on her own, but as men, we do not equip ourselves, because our masculine, and arrogant negative energy takes over, and we allow it. We'll walk away and leave a whole family behind, then beg to come back!

"WE'VE BEEN TAUGHT ABOUT THE LAW OF ATTRACTION, BUT NO ONE EVER TALKS ABOUT THE LAW OF DISTRACTION"

~ LEON R. WALKER JR~

PEARLS

- Work on your delivery. This is just as important, if not more, as your message.

- Ladies, an important pearl: never expect your man to check-in. It's definitely a nice thing to do, but don't pressure him into doing so. The more you lay off him, as regards your expectations, the more he'll be inclined to check-in. Some men have bossy mothers; you must know this from the beginning. If you're bossy, you'll tend to trigger your man and you'll *never* get him totally.

- Learn what emotional PMS is.

- Make sex so good that silent tears stream down her face.

- Learn how to say "I'm sorry," then explain why.

- Grab your man by the hand and take him away, anywhere. Don't always wait on him to take the lead; sometimes he doesn't want to. This is a role switch, and in doing so, we, as men, begin to feel what it's like to have our hands held, grabbed, and then be led; safely and unguarded. As you grab his hand, your man will not be inclined to follow. At first, he'll pull back; this is a natural reaction to us feeling like we're being "taken" or "forced," which we hardly accept. Hand-grabbing also suits the masculine female in a gay relationship.

- Dominance creates an imbalance. It starts in the head and goes to the heart.

- When a woman disconnects, her mouth closes before her heart. Her words are strong and powerful; she cherishes them but you're no longer worthy of her tongue

- When you leave a real, honest, and genuine relationship, the next one won't be. You left real because you were fake, so you'll get fake in return.

- Heal together. If you want help, first consult your husband or wife.

Chapter Twenty-One

Why Men Suffer - Relationship Vows

For me, I went into every relationship shallow, immature, unfocused, and not familiar with or practicing anything related to the elements that I discuss in Loveship! My imagination became my reality and my reality became my imagination. I had a *real image* that was based on a real, dysfunctional world. All of my future relationships would suffer because I didn't have any relationship vows--I wasn't prepared!

The divorce rate in the United States is 3.2, per every 1,000 people. One of the most common reasons for divorce is *"Lack of Preparation,"* going *into* the marriage. *Relationship Vows* are never spoken about although they are the root of everything that accommodates *Love Languages, Shadow Traits of one another, Growing and Climbing in love, Seasons and Reasons, Components of a Relationship,* and *Relationship Internship* which I speak about in the upcoming chapters. However, we plan, discuss, read over, become elated, and even share with our spiritual advisors about our marriage vows, but are they deeply connected to our corrected past, or just the excitement of our uncertain future? I mention these because they make up or identify either a current balance or what is out of balance or that which requires calibration. Most things that are out of calibration, have been so, for many years, leading up to being attracted to someone or searching for a potential partner. The relationship vows are a time for *re-setting, regrouping, revisiting* a moment in which the two of you focus and refocus on the intricacies of dating, relations, relating, understanding, undertakings, work life balance, and, but not short of, in-laws--which carries potential--*intergenerational transmission of family violence*, with reference to; past or current issues! Aspiring for a solid future. Even if, during the times of developing your relationship vows, it doesn't work, you are surely to avoid someone not living up to their wedding vows, later on. I truly feel that implementing *Relationship Vows* can and will reduce the quota of couples applicable to divorce. In doing so, you invoke many guidelines which equates to a precursor, ultimately developing hindsight before losing sight. I'm not saying that because you are intrusive with your *relationship vows*, in the beginning and throughout, that you will gain access to a happy marriage, however, exercising and knowing of each one's sentiments, with references to the relationship vows, you will tend to acquire a more quantitative transition that's indicative of marriage continuity, staying power and the avoidance of divorce by a much greater percentage. Again, and although the two of you may be working on and planning this marriage, according to the relationship vows, there is a chance that it *just* might not work, still! Please do not fret, because for one thing, we can't for a moment, forget reverting to an all knowing, and genuine, *friendship!* Doing so allows you to become completely aware of who this person really is and your knowledge base about them will improve immensely, for yourself, or someone you may desire later on or not. Relationship vows don't go away, nor do they end, yet they are the basis by which we engage in and with any human being, on all levels. This becomes a *Relationship Internship,* and in most cases, we have no idea this is taking place!

The genesis of suffering for most people is in hiding the truth, not "Presenting your past." Our suffering begins in our childhood; it did for me. Most women don't know our inner "Dark Child." In sharing this ugly secret, I felt that women would think that I was weak or even scared. Thinking this, in my mind, I wasn't strong but confused, and in her mind, possibly, I was weak, broken, and I feel like this is how she saw me. Because you don't know the real truth, you are left with *only* a hypothesis, that's it. You don't really know the truth, but I do. But in knowing the truth, and knowing that you don't know the whole truth, is strength to me--which caused a weakness in our relationship, leading to disintegration, disenfranchisement, and degradation. I was well aware of the demise before it happened.

I taught myself that my pain isn't something that I could share with anyone. I suppressed my pain and it made me feel stronger, knowing that I could still function in life and relationships, however weaker in that I didn't know how to express it. This is when I learned how to lie, deceive, and be dishonest and then believe it.

IN A TWISTED, WEAKENED STATE OF MIND, MY LIES AND HIDING GAVE ME A FALSE SENSE OF SECURITY, DUE TO MY OWN SELF MANIPULATION.

I was never groomed to be a groom and some young ladies aren't built up to be brides. Grooming and building women and young men to be brides and grooms start with writing your relationship vows, before marriage vows. We have only written wedding vows and this has been going on since the 1500s! If we take the time to write or discuss relationship vows—again, this is *not saying that the relationship will work*— we'll avoid additional atrocities such as lying, wasting time, red flags, broken promises, and more. The vows can be changed, altered, with sound adjustments along the way. Grooming and building to be a groom or bride starts with many intricate details, such as educating our kids and ourselves of knowing what a soul-mate is. Having or finding a soul-mate, you go from lonely suffering to chemistry, comfort, trust, to building, and then true love. In addition, we must learn the value of both men and women. Teach how "machismo" and "male chauvinism" can affect the relationship, and that women don't have to be docile, subservient, nor do they have to submit to male power— women have power too and it must be exchanged, equally. *Chivalry* is a definite must! Just as important, relationship vows should not be used for the wrong person, leading to a *relationship mismatch* and this comes to fruition when exercising the vows.

"Relate before you fornicate!"

~ Leon R. Walker Jr~

I did have great examples in my father, brothers, uncles, and cousins, however, I never heeded any relationship advice but I did focus on the good qualities that I saw in these men. Overall, they were all lovers of people, open and approachable personalities, too and for that, I am extremely grateful. The women in my family were also great examples. I come from a male-dominated family, so some aspects of life were masculine-influenced. I didn't learn to take advantage of the feminine side of my DNA until I got older. I wish I had done so, early in life. That would have surely made me a better boyfriend and husband. In my family, there were long marriages, and ultimately, the women became widows. There were also a few divorces and instances of cheating but, as a whole, I knew about longevity, staying power, and monogamy. They showed me that, yet I refused to make those a part of my relationships. I suppose that after knowing and experiencing great relationship practices, I chose to go the opposite way, against good morals, thus leading me to suffer. My father wasn't promiscuous nor was he a womanizer, although women loved and admired him. My mother wasn't promiscuous, either. Collectively, and after studying both parents, I can count on one hand, the women and men we saw in my parents life, with reference to dating. Neither of my parents slept around, so I developed this distasteful pattern, all on my own! That's not to say they weren't flirtatious, but the better qualities that my parents had, I ignored. I was not only a product of verbal abuse, but I was also shown that men ran the home without consultation of the women. I saw this with my grandparents and because my parents fought a lot, fear was instilled in me. I didn't learn to talk things out, my first reflex, when confronted with an argument, was to leave, walk away, or go get a drink, and by the next day, when it seemed that everything was back to normal, it wasn't.

I held onto those events and visions and for some odd reason, walking away resonated with me more. It was a pure form of *avoidance*! I ignored morals, to feed my demons.

This caused me to have abandonment issues as well. My mother was a great provider and leader, and so was my father, but since my parents started their divorce process when I was in the sixth grade, my morals for marriage ended. Just like a lot of other young men and women, *I never fixed my past,* thereby taking my childhood trauma into my future without seeking help, be it therapy or guidance. I held onto my anger and lack of relationship guidance in a profoundly closed-off effort to prevent myself from loving or being loved. So I didn't know, nor did I want to be embarrassed or embarrass myself, due to a lack of love knowledge, hence the deep suffering.

"OPEN UP TO REAL AND GENUINE PEO-
PLE THAT OPEN UP TO YOU—THEY KNOW
FULLY WELL THE HURT AND PAIN, AND
WILL NOT HOLD IT AGAINST YOU."

~ LEON R. WALKER JR~

My family values were drastically affected as well. This was when my "internal suffering" began. Not to mention, being molested and raped at such an early age, my mental state and mind development had been forged solely for lust, greed, selfishness, and being a mannish little boy, I was too mature, too soon. This forced me to skip over the intricacies of healthy relationships, thus basing all relationships with women on sex only. We groom our sons for sports, womanizing, to not cry, to be macho, and many more teachings. We miss the mark on healthy relationships, respect, honor, commitment, monogamy, and many more things.

It's a great practice to think about how you want to be, to and for your partner. Take in the good, bad, and the ugly, decipher it, understand them all, and get to know them, then make your decision, because we do have choices. The most unpopular ones are tougher to add to your daily regimen in healthy relationships because you're living right, spending time with family, honest, committed, and faithful. For some strange reason, living like this with your partner isn't favorable to your friends and some family members. They're either jealous, can't find the type of partner you have, or have never had proper "grooming." The easy choices are, for the most part, the ones we take on, so as not to be held accountable or be made to work hard in a relationship for future bliss.

The issue with young men and women today is that they want everything right now without taking the time to be patient, think things through, and communicate about if we're a match or not. This is why earlier, I mentioned that a relationship mismatch can be avoided, and so can cheating, heartbreak, letdowns, and stalking. Men suffer for the reasons that I mentioned but it can all be changed, worked on, improved, and avoided. Communicate and discuss—it's imperative! When you communicate with your partner and make plans to be together, once it reaches the ripeness for marriage, make sure to carefully write out, understand, take heed to, explain, be aware of, and practice living in your own wedding vows.

Two other forms of suffering for men are that some men are very well-versed in what immediate family means but the transition that's the hardest is trying to make your future wife and kids your immediate family, and your initial immediate family, come second. You can't please everyone, you must learn to smile and protect your family through it all! In my first memoir, *Broken, The Survival Instincts of a Child*, I discuss my dysfunctional childhood, in great detail. In doing so, I specifically discuss a male family member beating my mother up—knocking her front teeth out. Things like that should never happen. I saw that family struggle with the tension and the ability or inability to put husband or wife first. Not to take anything away from my dad, but we never knew why the family member did what he did, or why he got away with it. What is love? It's surely not beating a child's mother! From that horrifying, and tragic encounter, I was confused about primary and secondary family, but it became extremely clear to me, early on, to never hit women!

Not saying that my dad didn't put my mom first, but I wasn't educated on this. Thus, by living without knowing to put my secondary (marriage) family first, I eventually repeated my parents' divorce, twenty-eight years later.

Secondly, there's no way of knowing if your man was sexually abused, raped, or touched by a family member unless he tells you. However, I will tell you this. During and after every molestation, I was told to be quiet. It was always emphasized during molestation, and from that, for many, many years as an adult, I was silent during sex, coupled with a seveer lack in the ability to communicate about many things.

"WANTING LOVE OR WAITING ON LOVE SO BAD, WITHOUT LOVING YOURSELF, YOU LOSE YOURSELF, THUS BECOMING ILL FROM BEING HURT, SAD, AND LONELY AND WAITING. DON'T ALLOW YOUR PATIENCE TO MAKE YOU A PATIENT!"

~ LEON R. WALKER JR ~

I WANT TO KNOW WHAT LOVE IS

I want to know what love is.

Is love what I want to know? Only you know what love is.

I feel you, so I know you can teach me what love is.

I feel you, so I know I will find love,

what love is, love what, for what, love you,

to know what love is, that's what.

I want you to show me all about it,

it's all about what you show me,

then I'll know what love is, what love was, love was with you,

still with you, with us. With us, now I know what love is,

you and me, love you see.

Do you want to know what love is?

I mean, you know what it is, what it was,

what it can be, it can be special,

the love you taught me, yeah.

Love is waking up and seeing you in the morning,

yawning, knowing, that I just laid next to you all night,

yet happy that you are still here with me,

to share with me, the morning dew, to see

the sun as bright, as bright, as your beautiful face.

Love is… being with you, right here, right there,

everywhere. I'm safe, we're in God's grace,

that's what love is!

Let's Talk - The only love I knew and was taught of, was as a kid. Beyond that, all I could do was rely on my instincts of what I thought love was—being raped! Then finding out that it was lust and lust only. My parents did the best they could and they did great, but after their divorce, I never wanted my own family, ever again. Thinking that way would also keep me safe from knowing deep love, something I was afraid of. What does he want to know? For a sexually abused man, the easiest thing to ask, or know, or even want to know, is if you enjoy giving head or if you are horny.

Chapter Twenty-Two

Keeping a Man

Lesson Nineteen: Holding On

You can't keep a man if he doesn't want to stay—period!

"IF YOU ARE LITERALLY CHASING A MAN, THEN WHAT YOU REALLY WANT IS A BOY! BY THE TIME YOU'RE EXHAUSTED FROM CHASING HIM, HE'LL TURN AROUND AND MEET YOU WITH HIS 50/50, AND AT THAT POINT, YOU'LL BE EXCITED, LOOK DESPERATE, AND VULNERABLE. SCHOOLED, EDUCATED, AND MATURE YOUNG AND GROWN, MEN WILL FACE YOU. THEY WON'T RUN OR FEAR THE ISSUES AT HAND. LEARN TO KEEP YOURSELF, AND WHEN YOU DO, YOU WILL ATTRACT THE RIGHT MAN--THAT WANTS TO KEEP YOU!"

~ LEON R. WALKER JR~

More often times than not, women are taught to take care of their men. That's true but the lesson should be taught to both parties, but not at the cost of losing yourself. One valuable lesson that has been forgotten, is that while you are looking for a companion, teammate, lover, and confidant, be careful not to attract someone that's going to use and abuse you!

"WE ALWAYS TALK ABOUT OR WANT TO KNOW WHAT THAT OTHER PERSON IS GOING TO BRING TO THE TABLE. BUT IN SOME INSTANCES, WHAT THEY BRING TO THE TABLE IS THE INTENTION TO TAKE WHAT *YOU* BRING TO THE TABLE."

~ LEON R. WALKER JR~

Trying your hardest to keep him does one thing—it keeps him *away*. There will be too much added pressure and, in some cases, you're hiding your agenda, flaws, or true reasoning. He might be there with you physically but mentally, he's not. This is your way of "thinking" that you are providing top cover—a term I've heard pastors use. I'm not saying they're wrong, but if you keep that lid over him, he *will* boil over.

"EVERYTHING IN LIFE HAS DIREC-
TIONS FOR USE AND INGREDIENTS!
RELATIONSHIPS NEED THE SAME
AMOUNT OF CARE AND ATTENTION!"

~ LEON R. WALKER JR~

Example: Take preparing your favorite dish for instance. Let's go with collard greens. Black, Latino, Asian, and White people season differently. However, we all share a liking, nonetheless.

So you fill the pot with water (his/her body, soul) and every now and then, you check the temperature, remove the lid, take a step back to avoid the built-up steam billowing upwards, then proceed to add a little seasoning, maybe more water. Stir the pot, massage the greens, check the smell, smile, then put the top back on (The top being your new-found, aspect, view, knowledge, understanding, and plan to adjust to make the greens taste better). I don't care what you enjoy cooking, it still requires love, attention, and nurturing.

The last thing you do with the pot on top of the stove is to adjust the heat!

Now, back to what I was saying. If you keep your foot on his neck, you'll begin to suffocate him and he'll eventually explode. Women that perform in this manner have low self-esteem and trust issues, and in a lot of cases, it's not their fault. They either meet a man like me or will just stick to traditions.

Women born in the south have been taught to stand by their men, no matter what. I've come to find that this is very dangerous for both parties. The man knows this; therefore, he takes advantage of what she has been taught, knowing fully well that, in most cases, she'll never leave. The woman knows this as well; she'll remain, even after she's stabbed him for cheating!

"Don't ever enable a man because when you do, you allow him to become disabled, and at that point, you'll feel compelled to take care of him forever." You become his "disability check"

~ Leon R. Walker Jr~

If you have consistently pushed men away, this is a crucial time for you to sit back, think, and conduct your own *mental checkup*. When speaking to people informally, I change the terms that I use because they have become taboo, specifically mental health. Aside from mentioning going *"Inside The Box"* to better and find yourself, I also call it "Washing Your Brain" Do not confuse this with "brainwashing," as both work in totally opposite ways. "Washing your brain" is done by yourself, not by someone having a negative effect on you!

We rely on psychiatrists, social workers, and psychotherapists to examine us, give counsel, and recommendations. These are all helpful, but what we desire and how we can better ourselves, is always right there within us, both good and bad—*our parents' DNA*.

What has been passed down to you is obvious, and if it isn't, make it known to yourself.

Study your "who"—your mom, dad, grandparents, ancestors. Ask questions about them, what they did in life, how they acted and reacted. You may find that you act just like them, even the ones born in the early 1900s. In addition to going "Inside The Box," other things that worked for me and have given me peace, tranquility and a true life balance were first, controlling my addictions, so that when I did end my vice, I noticed a change in my behavior, eye white health, an increase in positive thoughts, slow reactions to evil, change in breathing rate, and I also became more reserved. As a man, determining my "Who" started by examining my dad. I found out that his dad didn't mention the word love, but he showed it. My dad was the same way, and so was I for many years, until I adjusted that.

This chapter, "Keeping a Man" has many variables to it, and that's why I explain different things about "Keeping a Man" which ultimately comes back to *knowing yourself.* Next, you have to venture out but focusing on keeping yourself and not someone that doesn't know themselves or their

DNA! If they don't know their DNA, you will find yourself wasting many years doubting yourself, trying to build up a person with a weak or fractured foundation, thus losing yourself and becoming unhappy!

"Washing Your Brain" is all about alignment, in many forms. Spend time in the sauna, watch what you drink, drink clean water, get into yoga (especially hot yoga), meditation, chakra, peaceful walks, 1.5 hour-long massages, calm, uninterrupted sleep, read good books, and have good conversations with like-minded people.

You may think that this doesn't have anything to do with "Keeping a Man." It does because by working on and building yourself up, you'll glow and attract from the inside out, and many things will occur. You will not worry about a man, your energies will fire on all cylinders, thereby warding off people that mean you no good and people that don't match your energy or positivity. The right people will end up in your circle and your force field, you'll become more into yourself, but one major thing will occur while "Washing Your Brain;" you'll never worry about how to keep a man any longer. The man that you do get will be conducting the same washing of the brain too, and will not want to ever leave!

When I attended the Air Force Leadership School in Montgomery Alabama, I learned many things and a lot of it has stuck with me. One thing that stood out was the concept of job mismatch: the wrong person for the wrong job. A lot of us are stuck in *Relationship Mismatches!*

Relationship mismatch becomes obvious for many reasons. To know if you're suffering

from a *relationship mismatch*, I'll name a few warning signs.

You will always have an odd feeling with that person.

Interests will hardly coincide.

Communication, most times will not be present.

Everything will seem forced.

Your days with that person will seem cold.

Your family will notice things.

There will not be much interaction with the kids.

Compliments, if there are any, will be very shallow.

Phone calls and text messages will be short or non-existent.

Health and appearance will fade.

Sitting away from each other on the couch.

Backs to each other while in the bed.

There will not be any showering together

There will be more attention shown to the animals in the house.

If you pack lunch for your partner, they will not eat it.

You'll feel like a stranger to his co-workers.

Back to what I began talking about, which is just as important. Don't make your current man suffer for the sins of the last man. When you do that, you make him better, but not for yourself—for her! The best way to fix this situation is to first *find yourself*. In finding yourself, you will find that you *are* in a relationship, but alone! In that relationship, there hasn't been any "relating," you're just a ship adrift. This is where you go from searching for your *Loveship* to finding your *Loneship!*

Sailing through life on a Loneship isn't necessarily a bad thing. It is however bad when you think that you've found the right guy, but after taking time for yourself, you'll notice that he never found you! Women also think that watching him closely is the right thing to do. It's not. Many things happen when you search and try to track him down.

First, you give away your private investigation when you change from the person you once were. You may think men don't notice, but we do. It's now in our best interest to focus on what you used to do as opposed to what you do now, in an effort to identify your pattern. You're always on the track for "her" man—I say "her" because if you don't know where he is, then you simply don't know who he is. One of the first things that go through a woman's mind when she thinks her man is cheating is the thought of another woman being better than you. Once you become insecure about "her," tracking him down goes from missing him, to trying to find him, to chasing, or even stalking "her."

I don't care what you own, how you treat him, or how good the sex and fellatio is, if he's not in tune or his life course isn't in sync with who you are and who he's not, he will not be able to process having a good woman when he has one, because he's not particularly a good man! On the outside, he'll look polished and ready to settle. However, on most occasions, the outer appearance, when well taken care of, becomes your trap. Nails done, car clean, facial hair trimmed up, he smells good, and is well-dressed— these are great qualities in a good man. As a woman, however, you must approach with caution and remain guarded.

"I look good, but I am not good!"

Don't ever chase me, ever! The crucial thing that will keep you safe is to ignore me about fifty percent of the time, which gives you fifty percent of yourself to fall back on. Some women give 100% immediately, therefore, you now belong to me with nothing to fall back on, aside from a dark hole that I created! Of course, when I walk into the club, bar, and sporting events, there will be lots of women that I attract. Those women are easy, and it feels good to be looked at like a piece of meat; it's flattering. For some of you, all you want is "meat" and not to "meet." The first woman who drapes herself all over me gives me her number before I even ask or remains all up in my face is the first one that I lose respect for and interest in. All she'll get is sex!

I might sleep with her but the sex will be emotionless. As bad as she's been craving a man to make love to her, it will not happen with me. During this phase, I'm still in the phase of adding up my "woman numbers" or building up my stable for the variety that I lust for and you just made it to number three for that week. I need a challenge.

Men respect women who can teach us. If you want to keep the man that you have, it's not hard. Some women struggle with this because, over the years, you've given everything up too fast, thereby exposing yourself too early (women are emotional—you believe this because society has made you) so you wear your heart on your sleeve and this makes you easily identifiable. It's okay to be emotional and passionate about relationships. I wish I was, years ago, but I wasn't. I'm not saying it's wrong, but what I am saying is being emotional isn't always a good thing because your soul is bared through your eyes when we talk. Should you hide things, remain reserved, hold back, and take precautionary measures? Yes, but more importantly, you must manage your sensory perception on all levels.

A man who says all the right things who, and in some cases, is able to back it up too can send nerve impulses to your brain, and your body, eyes, face, and facial expressions will react to it. During the meeting process or dating game, a great listener can be breathtaking. For the woman that meets the "Listener," he can be a great listener for many reasons, not all bad. This man just might be mature enough to take in and see your pain, hear your call for help, or even make you feel like you've known him for years. He will also be able to quickly process what you say or he may even pick up on what you might want to say—but do not.

Stop dumping all of your feelings and emotions on a man you've only just met. This makes you seem desperate, weak, and vulnerable. Feeling vulnerable, especially when you're drinking, will make you start to feel sorry for yourself, thus leading to a "One Night Stand." You'll pass that off as revenge on your ex or the current guy who's ignoring you and isn't satisfying your sexual needs. This isn't always the case though.

Some women just become fed up with crying, begging, and pleading then give themselves to a man because he "earned" you that night! The "Listener" usually earns that reward.

You have to pace yourself and the relationship. The more you see him grow and get into you, the more you release. We won't know the difference, really, but we'll become happier and happier. Like I mentioned earlier, we have the ratio, but you have the rations!

Just because you've been married for fifteen or twenty years doesn't mean that I am still happy or still respect you. You can't stay married just to out-do your parents or to reach your fiftieth anniversary. Marriage is a lifestyle, one of fun, happiness, and continued growth—and I failed at it miserably.

Every week, leave him alone for one to two days a week. He really needs and wants to miss you. You have to make him think, wonder about, and miss you without any drama. Slow down on the questions, don't mandate that he come home early. Wear new panties and stop getting mad. Spend more time with your friends so you'll see and discover why he enjoys spending time with his friends.

These will work because once you get him to be comfortable with you, he'll look for more love for you, and he has it in him.

A major mistake women make – and I know some of you will not agree with this – is thinking that they are men. I know you do your part in a relationship, the home, and other things, but so do we and we enjoy that, but please, never expect a man to pay for everything! When you do this, as hard as we work, our mindset becomes a thought of working just to pay for what she wants. No one wants to feel like they work for free, and although the money you expect from me takes care of the home, let me do it voluntarily! I shouldn't have to say "let a man keep his money" but I must. We enjoy being able to take care of business and we love providing but not because we have to.

Maybe there's an agreement in the marriage or relationship, but some of you complain about having a broke man. How do you think it feels to have a broke woman or to have money and have to give you all of it just because you think that it's supposed to be that way? Now he's broke because of you. When a man starts to change with his money, he is called stingy, selfish. You ask questions, accuse us of taking care of another woman, etc. While none of this is true, yet we feel compelled to hide money now!

Let me tell you two little secrets:

- When you think I'm broke or you do your best to try to keep, take, or manage my money, another woman who has her own money will want to give me money because she doesn't like how you drain me of my money. She had a man do her the same way, so we're both in the same situation, therefore, she can't wait to take care of me! I don't want her money, she doesn't want mine, and I'm not cheating, but it's a thought! Trust me when I tell you—it feels good to give a deserving woman money. Make yourself deserving by not expecting that I pay for everything!

- Once you relinquish control of a man's money, we'll be more inclined to do more for you, much more than we're doing with less money.

Now, in all of this, the man has to do his part, too and he arrives at this juncture in a few ways. He shouldn't be afraid to tell his boys how much he loves you. In addition, he has to make other women see and know this because there are women and men out there that will become jealous of your marriage. They will lie to come between you and your woman or man. He must celebrate and appreciate you often so that you do not have any reservations about forward movement.

Both of you must continue to add youth to your life; never become comfortable. When you become comfortable, you open yourself up to those waiting in the shadows, and they are. Marriage does not have to be a business; it must be fun each and every day. At the very least, if you're not doing anything, have a plan to do so later on. Give just as much time, energy, and thought to your partner, relationship, and marriage as you do to your job, the beer you like, and the sports or television shows you enjoy. Working out together is a time where you can help one each other, give pointers, and lift each up. This is a crucial time to get to know each other's bodies, aspirations, trust, unity, and soul. A lot of couples work out alone or with someone else; this can drive a wedge between both of you, attract other people, and/or allow one to outgrow the other.

"LISTENING AND RESPONDING WITH KNOWLEDGE, AND COMPLIMENTS—NOT ABOUT HER OUTFIT OR LOOKS—BUT ABOUT HER INTELLECT, IS A WAY OF MAKING LOVE TO A WOMAN'S MIND! SHE'S BEEN COMPLIMENTED ALL HER LIFE, SO SHE IS LOOKING FOR SOMEONE THAT SEES HER DIFFERENTLY. IT COULD BE SOMETHING SHE KNOWS ABOUT HERSELF OR NOT; EITHER WAY, WHEN A MAN NOTICES IT, IT'S VERY ENLIGHTEN-ING FOR A WOMAN."

~ LEON R. WALKER JR~

"I GOTTA LET YOU KNOW, YOU CAN COUNT ON ME, I'LL SET YOU FREE. I USE MY WORDS, CAREFULLY. IT'S GOING TO BE REAL, FORGET THAT FANTASY."

~ LEON R. WALKER JR~

SOUL PIERCING

I can't even concentrate, he went so deep,
I moaned so loud last night, but I was asleep.
I sat up in the bed, "Mommy *you ok?*" yes baby,
I'll be fine—I cried that day.
I lied to him, so easy and smooth,
I lied to him, just wanted him to move.
These are the moans that never come out,
he has no idea, what that dream was about.
You touch yourself, now you've got a chill.
Oh wow, you think to yourself, that felt so real.
He doesn't talk to you, like that man in your dream,
Oh shoot, sometimes, sometimes, I just want to scream.
You've gotten a piercing, so sexy and cool,
it is in your nipple, your temple, and running through—
now, what do you do. It's on the surface,
in your soul, you got it for him, it's on the surface.
It's temporary, and just for him, just for him,
just for him, now it's nothing to me, just for him.
That soul-piercing seemed so real, you see.
That's what I want, I want my soul, my soul,
my soulmate, he made me cry, girl he made me cry.
In my dream, damn, girl, he made me cry.
It was just his words, they seemed so true.
Just his words, they made me feel new.
Tired of feeling old, the next time I get a piercing,
I want it deep in my soul, deep, deep, deep, deep in my soul.
Soul piercing, I didn't know it exists.
Soul-piercing, now I can't resist.
I want my soul pierced.

Let's Talk- Shallowness has been around for many years; it's around now more than ever. Not just with women, but men too. We fix the exterior but we do not take much time on fixing ourselves on the inside. When you have a wonderful, caring, and loving soul, you'll exude extreme warmth, happiness, and the gentleness of a grounded human being. Most times, what we see is what appeals to us, and we feel what normally scares us.

For most people that are afraid of their "gut" feeling, we lose years, health, great relationships, confidence, self-esteem, and soulmates. Not until we are older, practice deep thinking, and become aware of who we really are and what we want, do we come to realize what's important to us, as far as connections go. We get so caught up in artifacts, material things, shallow people, and shallow times that our life just gets away from us, causing most people to settle. Some people are married just to be married, or are married but not in a marriage.

To the men: Something as small as looking in her eyes when you talk to her, rubbing her hand, giving her a compliment, the small things that we don't do often enough, will make a woman happy. An empty void is an empty woman. Remember, she's simple. You complete her yearning; you complete her. For some women, their happiness comes when their voids are filled. When their voids are filled, nothing else really matters. In some cases, they become stronger, their self-esteem goes up, their confidence increases, but it depends on a few things, as far as how the filled void will project her into the woman she wants to be. It also depends on how she was raised, what she saw her mother do, how her mother treated her father, this helps in her receiving of you.

Chapter Twenty Three

Appreciation

Lesson Twenty: Notice Her

In this world of plastic people, plastic surgery, fake lips, buttocks, breasts, and a host of other things, I have learned and really appreciated myself when I learned and began enjoying a woman for who she is, what she's gone through, and where she or we are going. Appreciation isn't just a word; it has *deep* meaning when used right and tied into why you appreciate her. There are many things that you can appreciate about a woman, but more so than anything, the most important thing about appreciation is how you show it. Keep in mind, I've been lacking on many occasions, and this is why I now know. First, let's talk about celebrating her, for whatever reason.

Celebrations should always be outside of her birthday or any holiday. This is when you take the relationship to another level. Celebrating her on a man-made holiday makes it seem like you're just following directions, according to national observance days; that doesn't mean much because the whole world is doing it, too. Do it when the whole world isn't doing it. Make it her time, all about her so that the whole world can see her smile!

There was a time when I hated buying cards. I made it quick and easy and it should have been a test of my true love and care for her—it wasn't, but it is now. The corner store or local gas station was my favorite. They always had those simple, or even dirty cards, just dangling from the rack or the one on the lower shelf. The one that no one wants but you, because you either forgot, don't care, or you're rushing—and it's collecting dust, too. That was the fastest way to get a cheap card. How disrespectful is it to choose something so unworthy of your better half? You can be creative on the computer; make a card with the kids (yours or hers) or take your time in the mall to find a card that fits her day. Either way, make it a very special project. Put time and energy into it, like you would something that really excites you; card buying should be fun and exciting too. It's ok to ask a woman at Hallmark for her ideas, suggestions, or advice. You'll see the excitement in her eyes, seeing a man put time into buying a card. The best card a man can buy is the "Just Because" card. These cards are and will always be a surprise, and they're supposed to be.

Don't ever just hand her a card, either. Place it where you know she'll look or have to go. The bathroom, by the computer, her car, her parent's house, and her job, after she leaves, so she'll have a nice surprise when she returns to work the next day. Two of the two most sexual and sensual ways to give her a card is walking up behind her while she's cooking and giving it to her or placing one under her pillow when the two of you get into bed. If you do it in the bedroom, put just a little bit of her favorite cologne on before getting in bed. The card, your nice smelling body, and you looking in her eyes after she opens *The Card* will earn you major points. You might have to call off work the next day!

"IF YOU'RE AN OPTION TO HIM, THEN YOUR OPTION IS TO NOT BE AN OPTION, THAT'S NOT OPTIONAL."

~ LEON R. WALKER JR~

THE CARD

He bought you a card, more than likely, he can't even explain what
it means.

He bought you a card, it has no feelings to it, just like other things.

You open it and read it, you give him a kiss.

It's your birthday, and all you got was this.

The card came from the nearest gas station,

"Oh baby, that's hallmark," he says without hesitation.

The words in the card, written by another man,

mean more to you than your current man.

He didn't even sign it, he hurried and gave it to you,

he knew damn well it wasn't a nice card.

You always settle, pleasing you isn't really hard.

He doesn't pay attention to you, no, not at all.

You got all cleaned up, ready to go out on a date,

he didn't even know; the card was a day late.

Cards mean so much, he knows this is true.

It's always been him, him, him, he never thinks of you.

How long will you take it?

It's to the point now, you just fake it.

He has no clue, no clue at all,

yeah, go ahead and cry, she can hear you, the lady in the next stall.

Yeah, it's your birthday, your anniversary,

and you're thinking, he never says these words to me.

That card, you get one every year. That card

especially, especially not special, it's your day for it.

There were times you had to give him the money just to pay for it.

This should be easy, it's just a card. Yeah, that's how he feels about it.

Giving you nothing, it isn't hard, just like the same old, meaningless,

thoughtless, fruitless, emotionless, thankless, senseless,

gas station card, on the *wall*, dresser,

table, your purse, and you have the nerve to keep them all!

Let's Talk- Women hold onto things, they cherish even the smallest, cheapest things. They mean more to him than it does to you. You hold on and never give in or give up until it's time. As men, we have no time-piece in our minds; we forget important days, dates, and moments. In most cases, our moral compass is off, causing our inability to not only relate but recalibrate when we are "morally off." This immensely compromises our way of thinking, and more importantly, connecting.

In some of my relationships, I didn't care what I bought or when I bought it. Those were the times when I knew the relationship was over, probably long after she knew! I am a very giving person, but when the relationship wasn't about anything but sex, I didn't care at all. Most women will settle, accept anything on special days, just to prevent themselves from crying or being hurt.

You ALWAYS go out of your way to give him nice things on special days; you'll even buy things for his kids, knowing his ex doesn't like you. You hold on for as long as you can, even taking a back seat to his mother, and in some cases, his ex. His ex knows this. You do your best to make good out of a bad situation, like being dealt a crappy hand at a poker game, you still try to find the good in the relationship. I applaud you for that, but it says a lot about your current state of mind when you do that. Either way, I salute you!

Chapter Twenty Four

Child Support

Lesson Twenty-One: Just Don't

I was a cheater and it cost me $320,000.00 in child support! My divorce took nineteen months and cost me $11K!

I had to go through this, not because of punishment, but God made me see that I spent too much time living in what *other people* influenced me into, instead of residing in what my grandparents, parents, aunts, uncles, brothers, and mature, committed men, taught me, monogamy!

Child support is usually a product of cheating, that's why I'm telling my story about it.

Between 2000 to 2006, I was promoted from Chief to Senior Chief to Master Chief, and finally, Command Master Chief. Although these are all very significant promotions with increased responsibility, authority, and of course, pay, I only received a very small amount, if any. When I did receive the financial increase, that too was ultimately removed. Don't ever get upset with the mistress; the anger should be directed toward you and your penis.

My promotions *were not* commensurate to the amount the work I put into attaining them, however, the reduced amount was a consequence of the work I put into hurting those I hurt!

People *must* realize that karma doesn't wait but it does attack you when you are just as vulnerable as you made those other women. Right when you think that you've gotten away with, you'll find out that you never will. Child Protective Services withdrew my paycheck instantly and also sent me a letter. **CPS** are the first letters you see when you open their correspondences! Trust me, you do not want to receive a letter like that! My mind kept telling me that all I worked for was in vain. I tried my best to keep going (I eventually pushed through) but like most men, we become angry with the woman that we cheated with as if she made us have sex with her.

She might have enticed you, led you along, but when you're married, engaged, or in a relationship, even if it's not a healthy relationship, do not add another person until you are both free from one another. By adding another person to your relationship, you're adding sex demons. Sex demons come with odd feelings, different body odors, and unpleasant sex. I lived that life too, for many years. You may think you're getting away with it or doing something right, but you'll surely get a BPR—Bad Penis Report!

"Girllll, he's big down there, but I'll pass next time. His body stinks, I couldn't even enjoy it. Old stankin' ass!"

Women know when you are cheating, believe this!

When cheating, you spread yourself very thin and become unable to perform in many ways, not just sex. You'll be spread so thin, that you will not be able to keep up with things you once did with the family. You're doing your best to hide the other woman, her text messages, requests, time spent with her, the movies, gifts she wants, holidays, a lot. She'll eventually want to replace your woman or wife, even if at first, she says she's down with being the "other" woman. I'm speaking from all that I have done and not been able to do and only to warn you. Women hate being kept a secret, especially if your woman, fiancée, or wife, isn't a secret!

You can't be married and treat another woman just like your wife.

I made all of them feel like they were more important than the next, and when they realized they weren't, I tapped into their anger that they didn't know they had. That's when you wind up on the I.D channel or the television show, Snapped!

Why did I cheat?

Because I lacked morals and didn't or couldn't care about just one woman. Each woman had something that I liked, more than the next one. I was more comfortable with having a variety in many women, as opposed to having it all in one woman. Two things that played a crucial part in my cheating were greed and lust, but here are more:

- Being a player was more popular than monogamy
- The woman stops trying to better herself but only because I couldn't motivate her.
- Greed
- Lust
- Looking for someone that we can dominate so that we can't be held accountable.
- Unresolved, *identified* childhood issues.
- I wanted to try new things on many women, I got bored with the same sexual exploration of the same woman. Most of them responded differently and that took my confidence to extremely higher levels.

How could I care about so many different women, you may ask? Well, first, I didn't care about myself, so how could I care about any of them? My interest wasn't about them, it was all about what I could possibly get them to be interested in, how far I could stretch their mind, especially the ones who told me no. Those were the ones that, in my mind, were begging to be taken. I made myself think that saying no was a test for me to make her comfortable with the most bizarre, or extreme measures, even if it caused some sort of danger. As a child, I was close to losing my mind. I wanted to see exactly how that looked on a woman's face, in a fun way. If she kept going with whatever I recommended, I became really turned on!

From end to beginning. I want you to think of this, before you cheat, I want you to see, feel, and perspire from thinking forward about what you could possibly be heading into, if you delve into infidelity. When imagining the end before the beginning, you will now experience fear, sickness, sadness, and hopefully, a change of heart.

Reverse the feelings and thoughts of what happens when you cheat:

I could not imagine my girlfriend, wife, or fiancée coming home and telling me she's pregnant by another man, or I find out when she delivers! This is the shit I took women through.

- Being stalked

- Being run off the road

- That person goes to your job or home

- Imagine another man rubbing your woman's stomach, with his and her child in her womb, not yours, yet you see her daily.

- Think about it the other way too—you rubbing the other woman's stomach that has her and your child in it, and not yours and your wife's!

- Emails, text messages, social media blasts

- Every pay raise goes to CPS

- Acid or hot grits being thrown on you

- The other person hurts your spouse or fiancée

- Embarrassing family and in-laws

The price of cheating takes a lifetime to pay back. Either your conscience will haunt you, or she'll constantly remind you of it, or you'll see the man she cheated with, or you might pass a venereal disease! Everyone gets hurt; some recover, some don't. Most men try to keep it a secret, especially if the woman that they cheated with gets pregnant and has their child. They planned for the baby to be a lifelong secret until your wife receives a letter from the other women, like it happened with me!

In Chapter 15: "Shattered Heart," Chapter 16: "Night Stalker" and Chapter 17: "You Ain't Leaving Me," you will notice a dark and twisted pattern. A pattern that I was very much aware of because I sought revenge by any means necessary.

Unbeknownst to me, that mindset was not only from the devil (whom I chose to blame) but was also part of my mental illness. There are many things that reside in mental illness—for me, I believe two of those traits were: being vindictive, with the inability to process hurt or pain, when projected onto other people, in order not to become emotionally involved with that person and secondly, being vengeful—in my case, towards women!

Why do I mention mental illness when the chapter is clearly titled "Child Support"? Well, because many facets lead to you paying child support; *cheating, abuse, neglect, relationship mismatch,* and *jealousy* (a person's anger towards having to pay child support and then watching her look better and better or when she finds a man that's much better than you.) Jealousy isn't hard-wired to our brain but it is a *shadow trait.* And during times of anger, stress, hurt, and jealousy, you may forget about child support and begin seeing doctors for mental illness (hurt feelings)!

"Doc, it's not about the money, but I finally realized that I do love her"

The mental illness is real, I'm not saying that it isn't. However, not only does it stem from reduced paychecks, which causes stress and a lesser quality of life, but you now wonder if his penis is bigger and better than yours, and women have a way of making us believe this. *Hurt ego!*

My mother received child support but since I didn't tell my parents about my abuse, I had no support in dealing with my issues as a child. Just imagine a child molested and raped by three women on separate occasions and not getting help for it through the years. Imagine always referring back to your anger when hurt by a woman in your latter years, thus leading you into a life of disdain.

I've read about and watched bitter and angry men like myself on television, who ultimately became serial killers. In my case, due to the unresolved issues of childhood, I had become a serial cheater. Outlined below was my path to destruction:

Childhood issues—promiscuity—instability—emotional detachment— abandonment issues—infidelity——child support!

Years later, after six to seven months of therapy, I wasn't diagnosed with narcissism nor was I a psychopath. However, I did possess those traits. For one, I was severely unstable with reference to unhealthy relationships. Did the psychiatrists or social workers misdiagnose me or was I just so cunning that I manipulated their questions and tests? Either way, I did find it in myself to self-diagnose so that I could better my mental health.

You need to be mentally healthy to function in a relationship, or else bad things happen and you may not be able to relate, making you angry rather than understanding and working it out. I never wanted to work things out, instead, I wanted it my way or the highway, one that I took myself on. I was always a relationship flight-risk!

When you plant something in your mind and act on it, it becomes premeditated, and takes on a life of its own. In 1992, after leaving San Diego and canceling a marriage, premeditating and childhood trauma, for me, led to unprecedented levels of unkind gestures. The seed planted was my goal to hurt women, break their hearts, and to never, ever commit—ever again. As with everything that's "Pre" and not well thought out, *there will be many people left in your wake, caught in your atrocities* who will suffer. My mischievous ways, coupled with a sick mental state of mind, led me to focus on feeding my *broken*, little, child-like anguish, instead of repairing a current relationship and becoming predestined.

Men and women get angry about child support. In some cases, the accuser is at fault, however, the anger can still be traced back to their childhood, and here's why:

Until you get over your childhood anger, be it losing your dad or mom, being evicted from your home, being broke, having money or your family's home (divorce) forcefully taken from you, specifically admitting the wrong-doings which led you becoming divorced, etc., child support will always piss you off. You'll see it as a personal loss or defeat in life.

Being morally inept, a lot of us repeat what we went through as children. I and many others have vowed to never leave home, get married, or be hurt by a significant other, but when we repeat anything related to us being a "product of our broken environment" (which I was), then we begin to go down that road of dysfunction, the self-pity, or, for the narcissists, wanting others to feel sorry for us!

Since we didn't do right and now have to pay, we feel like paying child support is unfair and has nothing to do with the relationship.

"Man, we're divorced but why she put me on child support? She know my moms left me when I was a kid and shit!"

Then we get political

"She gon' let a white man dictate how much money I pay her—my mom did my dad like that!"

Most times, the anger isn't about child support. It's more about the secret woman "telling" on us and getting us caught.

As for me, I never thought of cheating as being unfair. That was the first clue that I was a narcissist—maybe you are too. In my mind, I had a right to cheat because she wasn't satisfying me—how sick is that?

I was one-dimensional and one-dimensional men will blame women for everything, including things we don't know about or how to do; it's either her fault or our mothers' fault. Women are *three dimensional*, they see all before we do and in most cases, we're not ready for either dimension, thus causing anger, embarrassment, or shame.

Don't avoid finding out if you're a narcissist or you'll face a situation that will cause you to pay and lose out, again and again.

If you are not fair and honest in your own diagnosis, especially when you're the perpetrator, disrupting and breaking up the family, child support will feel unfair and piss you off for years! You have to break the family cycle, both men and women.

Lesson: The root cause of your problems isn't normally the current husband, wife, or fiancée (I mention fiancée because that's the stage I started cheating), it is you, over and over again, sadly. In my case, I hadn't fixed anything internally, leading me to hurt innocent women. I saw the world from the inside out and not the outside in.

You may not be the cause of the divorce; however, you may just be in a "relationship mismatch," which I'll discuss too. Identify this problem and move on, no need to continue hurting someone that you're not honest with. During my downward spiral, I never came to terms with myself about my atrocities (Avoidance).

Due to my self-neglect, I was a distraught, overweight Naval First Class Petty Officer. Cheating almost cost me my career. In 1995, when it all happened, I weighed 190 pounds. During my time in Recruiting (1992-1996), I was Recruiter of The Quarter and Recruiter of The Year. I was successful only because I was good at what I was doing and Cleveland loves, believes in, and supports the military. But morally, I was a piece of shit during those years!

In one year, due to the self-imposed stress, my body fat increased from four percent to thirty-three percent, and I now weighed 245 pounds, well over the Naval standards so I was counseled about it. My drinking increased drastically and my interest in life dwindled fast. It was recommended that I diet, seek help, and add my daughter to my page 2, a page in our service records that annotates those that are dependent on us. I never did that either. I had a secret that I told a female friend about-- we were really cool, up until the Page 2 was mailed to my house, while I was out to sea!

"Yo man—who mailed paperwork to my house?"

"Probably your girl, you know--your little buddy, she has access to our records, plus she likes you and knows that you are in a relationship—I heard she gets down with women—too!"

As her friend, we were strictly platonic, but she'd always comment on how beautiful my family was, however--since her son's father kept their child a secret, too, and I took up for him, I must have been a trigger for her.

"People will come to you with their problems just as long as you don't make them feel like they're a problem."

~ Leon R. Walker Jr~

YOUR GIRL

She watches you, she knows you better than your man

Tell her what you want, all she's thinking is *"girl, I can."*

You need to vent, you need to express.

Let's go out for a drink, she picks out your dress.

She's there to help you, she's there to listen, she knows you're in a mess,

that's why she picked out that beautiful dress.

She knows you better than your man, she feels your every pain.

Outside, she watches you cry, you tried to hide it, even through the rain.

Girl, let's go out to eat, he'll watch the kids.

She's slowly replacing him,

just like *HER* girl did.

Damn he can't, damn he can't, girl, he just can't understand me.

Girl I can, I can, as she looks at you, drinking her tea.

Does she want him, does she want my man?

is all you think, yea she wants my man.

I can't let her know, I can't let him go, let him go,

let her know, oh, that's *"my girl,"* she helps me grow, grow, grow, grow.

Or does she want me to go, grow away?

She told me, just the other day, oh yeah,

my girl helped me in this way.

It's funny how you say,

"He just doesn't understand me, no, not at all,

he's not feeling me," yet you pray, pray, pray,

for just another day, you want him to stay.

Girl please, please, please, stop talking that way,

are we still cool if I let him stay? Yea, yea, we cool, let him stay,

I'm your girl, each and every way,

that's my girl she would say, that's my girl, each and every way.

You toast up high, your smile is wide, hmm, I can't stay, there's no way.

He doesn't understand me, he doesn't feel me, and I complain every day.

Is it enough for me to stay, pray, go away?

I'm so confused, and not just today.
Girl I can, I can, we can, we can find you a man.
You cut your eyes, but never say a word.
It doesn't matter though, her admission was heard.
Your girl is there, in each and every way,
he'll be gone, but she'll stay.
Her touch isn't enough, a hug, a kiss, just girl stuff.
He told you she likes you, it has to be true.
All he had to do was like you too.

Let's Talk - A lot of men don't understand women who like and understand other women. I will tell you: there are men who are jealous of your relationship with your female friends. Some would rather you have a male friend, because a male friend, in most cases, does not understand the intricacies of a woman's touch, thoughts, reactions, wants, or even her needs, nor can they replicate it. This thought process makes a man comfortable with a man being around his woman, in quite a few cases. This is prevalent in those men that DO realize that they can't measure up to a woman. Some men can, but the ones who can't are more comfortable with a man being around his lady.

Ninety percent of the time, this stems from a man's insecurities within himself. He'll make things up in his mind and then start to believe it. "Your girl," being on the outside, is more able to observe everything you're going through. She has patience, hindsight, she's fair, unbiased, understanding, with a clear vision. However, there are exceptions because there are women who will hate on your man because he's treating you right when she's not being treated right, so be careful with her and what you tell her.

"A LOT OF WOMEN GIVE THEMSELVES TO SOMEONE BECAUSE THEY HAVE YET TO TREAT THEMSELVES WITH THEMSELVES."

~ LEON R. WALKER JR~

PEARLS

- Looks can and will lie about a person's soul.

- When you cheat, the universe will hold you accountable. If you cheat again, the hurt partner will extend injuries to you—physically, financially, or spiritually (because at the time of hurt, the devil plays an integral role in their decision-making. This is in addition to their damaged heart, lack of willpower, and broken moral compass). They'll ask forgiveness and receive it, then move on and heal and you could possibly be sued for "emotional distress."

- Always consult your 'relationship" vows during the relationship and marriage. This will allow you to revert during the courting stages and remind you why you like or even began to love one another. Sometimes people change during a relationship and don't know why. In some cases, it's external—a job, family, or even human, negative influences from broken people that want company.

- Stop thinking that you have to control everything. This applies to both parties. When you do this, you make your partner feel inadequate and they will look to other people for validation and reassuring confidence, which could turn into them liking that other person, including their counselor!

- Ladies, if he loses an erection while you are playing with his testicles, never play with them again. Some men like this and some don't. You need to know this well beforehand.

- Your name may be *Jim*, but her vagina isn't a *gym*! It's not a workout down there, so take it easy, buddy! If you treat the vagina right, talk to it, cultivate it, it'll perform for you every time—it has a mind of its own but open to your vibe, care, and tenderness.

- Your name might be Jenny, but her vagina isn't associated with Jenny Craig, so remember, homegirl—you have one too!

- Before you plan to have sex with someone that you truly are into, or enjoy, fill your body with less-acidic fruits and drink lots of water. A solid week or so, will do. Sweet taste is a turn on. Stay away from ribs, gizzards, collard greens, garlic, and definitely— asparagus!!!!! This is for both partners. Some men get so excited for the special day, they won't even check their "orange" urine before she arrives.

- Ask her and him if pubic hairs bother them. The coarse ones sit on the back of your tongue and are hard as hell to get off. A small break is needed to retrieve it. The not-so-coarse ones slither all the way down into your stomach, long and silky, but irritating as hell! They come out like a tapeworm.

- Sometimes, go to dinner and the movies by yourself.

Chapter Twenty Five

Mommy/Daddy

Lesson Twenty-Two: The Single Masculine Mom and Dad with Gay Children

This next chapter is just as important as any other chapter because it deals with kids. With kids, how you raise them, deal with, and handle them can and will affect any and all of their future relationships, and this is why I am talking about kids in Loveship.

Some moms and dads are put in this predicament making them assume an additional role. It's not easy; you may even worry at times. Being overprotective, overbearing, or too intrusive will push children away, eventually. Even if your husband or wife has left, is in jail, or deceased, you're still a woman/man and a mother/father. To act like a lady, more often than acting masculine, plays a key role here, and for dad, not too masculine. Yes, you may have to fill the role of dad/mom, however, you can only do so much— you must include a mentor, in your children's life, period!

Your son or daughter may or may not want another person in the house, and this is understandable because they'll still desire their biological parents. It will require a man and a woman who understands this—one that is nice, approachable, or has gone through this as well. They'll understand how to approach your children, how delicate they are, based on their childhood experiences—if you so select someone to be in your child's life. Please know that it is important that they have strong, confident, and passionate figures to talk to, bounce ideas off of, share his/her secrets, build confidence, tap into their masculine/feminine sides, share their pain, ideas, and thoughts on life, but they must also *not* be homophobic—this has to be clear from the *get-go*!

Some sons are okay with the masculine mom, but the main and more understanding one is the gay son. You must recognize this or he'll be abused by his boyfriend, thus the need for a male figure being around to talk and remind your son of his masculinity. This will offer him protection and will also give him a sense of security—confidence. Men, gay and straight, are abused too and need to know how to deal with it or draw the courage to stick up for themselves.

Having gay children is not a problem. They are who they are, and in most cases, will become very confident and mature early on. Understand them and do not fight against how they feel; you don't know their feelings until you talk to them. You must be very approachable and always listen first. If you must respond, do it only when asked. Soliciting advice will make your child feel like they're a problem or have a problem and this will make them defensive before anything else. Be patient, careful, extremely cordial, and treat them as the regular human beings that they are.

Do not force him/her to go to counseling—if you do, they'll shut down on the counselor, and you, most times. You can't make them feel like outcasts. Don't keep them away from family, they have to not only feel loved, but more importantly, feel understood, respected, wanted, cherished, and appreciated! This applies to the heterosexual son, the father raising his daughters alone, and all parents, both gay and heterosexual alike. In the case of a dad raising daughters, you must find a woman that knows well through her life experiences. I must warn you though, through my reading, research, and my experiences as a child, knowing now from my interviews and therapy, statistically—ninety percent of children that have been raped, molested, or fondled, have been abused by people they know and trust, so be extremely careful who you select. Do your research and background checks.

After all that I have discussed with you, we must talk about meeting the parents. In most cases, the father gives his daughter away. However, for many—and I do mean many—years, mothers have not given their sons away. For whatever reason, dads do the giving away and mothers do the bringing back or never letting go of her son. Some do let go, but most do not—for many reasons too. Mothers holding onto their son has been a problem in many relationships, and marriages. But more so than anything, sons holding on to their mothers have been just as bad.

Meeting the parents is crucial in any relationship. Some sons avoid women who are like their mothers while others look for women who are like their mothers. Young ladies do the same with their dads.

The sons who *avoid* women like their mothers (masculine moms) have a certain disliking for their mothers, ways, thought processes, or are just ready to get away from her "overbearing, and controlling" ways. In this type of mother-son relationship, your son will go through many women before you meet any of them, if you meet them at all. This is the young man who wants to be a man and not a mommy's boy. He'll listen when his mom talks but will surely tune her out, just like a scorned husband. He has seen how you treat your husband and doesn't want any part of it. Normally, these women repeat themselves around the house, thus poisoning her children with her values, traditions, and beliefs. I'm not saying that the mother is wrong, in any way, however, she must be careful not to overcompensate with her directing.

She thinks her way is the only way. She learned that from her mother or had a father who just took a backseat and gave in to everything the mother wants. This woman, in some cases, never received the teachings of a man. Although she may admire her dad, most of it comes from him being passive, which is more convenient for her and her mother to run the household. Comfort, not confidence has been bred, here!

For the father raising his daughter, he may have a bad habit of treating her like his son, if he has one. If he doesn't, he will still infuse his masculine ways into his daughter. By doing this, the daughter will look at men in a different light. She'll love, enjoy, or even lust after men, but her ways and her lifestyle will be just as rough as a man's. Daughters like this make it hard for men to love them because she didn't receive her nurturing ways from her mother, for whatever reason.

Women who despise their husbands and have either remained married or have become just roommates will not trust them with what he says to the children. She is on the leading edge of reprimand! Her displeasure with how he hasn't performed as a husband resonates deep in her soul and nothing he says or does will matter. Often, she'll feel like she has to "undo" everything that the kids dad has said or done, thus thoroughly confusing her children, young ladies alike. Whether she knows it or not—most times she doesn't—this type of mother is more in touch with her masculine side, while being guarded!

Let me tell you a secret, ladies. Your son may never tell you, but these young men hold their fathers in high regard and he can't do any wrong in their eyes. Some of you know this and can't stand it. When you provide too much top cover, you brainwash your son into believing that everything you say is true and right. A son in this type of relationship with his mother will begin to question everything his woman or wife says. Furthermore, co-parenting has been destroyed. The husband or ex becomes simply a bill payer!

Lesson Twenty-Three: Mr. Hubby—Hold On

The man or husband who holds on to his mom does so for many reasons. Yes, you should have a close and healthy relationship with your mother, but remember you are not the Little Poo-Poo, Bubby, Nuck-Nuck, Lil Boosie, Tay-Tay, Lil Tank, or June Bug you once were. This man goes to mommy so that she can agree with everything he says.

We all need and want reassuring confidence, but not the type that provides a false sense of reality. He visits his mom often, and more so while he's at his lowest point. They can reminisce about old times, school days, family, and even the girlfriend that his mom and sister could control. Sadly, they are intimidated by a *strong woman*, for many reasons, but the main and most probable reason is that his new, strong woman won't take their shit. She won't allow them to borrow money like the weak ex-girlfriend did! The new, strong woman puts a stop to all childish things in an effort to build with her man. During this time, the man doesn't see nor understand her method, thus going against her every plea and attempt. Before long, she'll slowly let go because she already knows her worth, and therefore, move on, leaving "Mr. Hold-on" to live his life out with his mother and sister.

Also, the mom and sister will recognize when their son/brother is moving away and breaking that vicious cycle. They won't like it—if he does break away!

Some men are well-acquainted with the meaning of the immediate family, but the transition that's the hardest to make is trying to make your wife, the immediate family and making your initial immediate family come secondary!

"FIND YOUR PASSION IN YOUR LIFE,
THEN FIND LIFE IN YOUR PASSION."

~ LEON R. WALKER JR~

Chapter Twenty Six

The Preacher Daddy

Lesson Twenty-Four: The Father That is Not

Father Not - There are many twists and turns in a father who preaches every day of the week. Some are legit while some are not. I have also met some that were counselors while being cheaters, overbearing, and dishonest. The types who counseled married couples and then took the wife away from the grieving husband.

As a man dating the "preacher's" daughter, you must stand your ground. This is by no means meant to be disrespectful, however, the daughter won't see any wrong in her father expecting *you* to live like *he* lives or how *they* live. In some cases, the daughter and mother may have forgiven the preacher father for his infidelity and they'll forgive you too. However, the fact remains that you're not her father, so be you.

Once you stand your ground, there will be a disconnect in your new (primary) family; you'll notice a gradual pulling away by them, away from you. The easiest thing to do is to jump on board and the hardest thing to do is to break away, keeping your dignity but losing a potential wife. The only man that she'll find is one who will cave into her father's whims—one that will commit. Once he commits, he'll lose a lot of himself and struggle in the relationship. Caving in will cause him to be fake around a family that lives in their values and doesn't value his. Yes, we all make mistakes, but as we grow and learn, we should discontinue our controlling thoughts and practices as well, especially if we're the ones who almost destroyed the family.

The man that enters this type of family will not see eye-to-eye with the father, and on many occasions, this will hurt and make you uncomfortable. You will seem to be at odds with or an outcast to her family.

As a preacher dad, he must take heed to past misfortunes; some fathers do and some do not. I am not a preacher but have experienced what I am telling you. Some have regained their good-natured life, through real divine intervention, to get back on track.

Lesson Twenty-Five: The Father That Is

Father is - Both kinds of fathers possess a sense of understanding but the one who is the most reasonable, understanding, clear-minded, and more humble of the two is the one who understands the most and doesn't force his will on you. His teachings, just like those of the "Father Not," are teachings, but will also convey his long-healed heart and not one that "*expects*" you to cave in or do what he says, only. His love for his daughter also feeds his fear of her getting hurt. This father can see you for who you are and also wants to know where you plan to take his daughter, just like "Father Not."

However, this father isn't just manly or masculine, nor does he rule with an iron fist. He knows women, not from a sexual sense, but from their perspective. It's essential to spend time speaking with this type of father. You'll be compelled to, simply because he makes you feel comfortable. He goes out of his way to do this because he has been in your shoes before and totally understands how it feels to be uncomfortable. "Father is" doesn't take a front or backseat, he knows all the roles—himself, his wife, daughter, and you—he's a well-rounded man. His forgiving heart is his best trait and you'll not only see this, but you'll feel it too. This "Father Is" will not struggle to keep things together, he is truly a "Glue Guy." Whereas the "Father Not" still holds reservations and regrets about his past infidelity, and at times, the regret will find its way back into his mindset! You must know both types of fathers, intimately!

Lesson Twenty-Six: Twenty-Fifth Anniversary Mom

A mother who has been married for a long time—ten, fifteen, years or longer—will expect nothing less from you. Monogamy is what she knows and believes in. She may have fornicated so she understands but doesn't recommend it. Either way, you must have a sit down with her. She'll expect it, so never avoid it; do this immediately. Hiding or shying away will reveal red flags. It is imperative that you do not try to make friends with her right away; it has to be natural. Moms can and will pick up on everything and will discuss it with her son or daughter when you leave. Never avoid family functions. Be social, respectful, and don't remain stuck to the son or daughter all the time during the function; you have to mingle. If you start doing house chores for mom, you shouldn't stop.

"A REAL PARTNER LIVES BETWEEN YOU AND THE WORLD."

~LEON R. WALKER JR~

Loveship *Loveship*

PEARLS

- If he hugs you and cuddles after his orgasm, and you don't have to ask for it, he's special.

- If you still have butterflies when you see someone, after not seeing someone for the past five, ten, or even fifteen years, and you parted on good terms, you might want to consider being with that person if the both of are still single. He or she is surely a soulmate.

- Men are package deals, too.

- A psychopathic or narcissistic man or woman will make you put your life and heart on the line. There is nothing you can do about them in this state of mind until they decide to get help, most won't because they're in deep denial. You must become acutely aware of their traits as soon as you can and start to take care of yourself immediately upon your discovery of their actions. You have nothing to do with his or her upbringing, genetics, or DNA, yet you try your best to help revive such a damaged person. During your acts of resuscitation, you lose time, develop health issues, and begin to doubt yourself, amongst many other things. They need you more than you need them!

- If a man says he's busy, leave it at that. On many occasions, contrary to what you're thinking, he just might be out buying you a gift. Don't spoil it. Some people remain obstinate due to lack of effort in their past relationship by their partner, by not giving yourself or the next person a chance to experience new ideas, better character traits, or a higher level of respect for you. Busy isn't a secret nor is it a means of disrespect.

- Before you marry someone, know how they live, not just where they live.

213

- Acting like the kid that was never fixed, buys us time in a relationship.

- When you consistently give people a break, they will break you.

- Some men fear better in their life.

- Focus on the key and not the lock. We have mental blocks and locks and instead of being angry about why our mind is locked, use your key to unlock our mindset. Do you know what your key is?

Chapter Twenty Seven

L-2

Lesson Twenty-Seven: Love and Leadership

"MY MAN..WE ARE LIKE CLAY, BEFORE SHE TOUCHES US! LIKE CLAY IN A WOMAN'S HAND, SO IS THE MAN OF HER DREAMS."

~ LEON R. WALKER JR~

Women love and lead from a totally different perspective. We know this but do we ever consider it when it comes to understanding them? I never have despite knowing that women felt and thought differently, yet I didn't even put much thought into that. This is a constant mistake that I made. I learned that women want to mold and sculpt a man into one of their dreams, and not control you because of who you are.

As men, we never speak of "a woman of our dreams," at least I didn't. The molding begins when they see potential in us and as she does, her intentions are to make us equals and develop our life course to ensure synchronization and balance—I never saw this! We both have strengths; she may know something that I don't and I may know or have something that she doesn't.

Her cautionary senses are heightened and extended as protection of our assets—to avoid distractions and being misled by jealous people, friends and family included! She's much more aware in the beginning because she doesn't like to waste time nor does she rush into anything. This is her Love and Leadership combined, just in case we become "unequal" for less fortunate reasons. A woman leading a man is merely course-correcting and shall be respected and not thought of as anything other than that. Spiritually, she knows that she has come from and is made from man. She also knows that she must re-enter our bodies and minds to heal and continue to be a part of us, so that we may continue to become a cohesive unit!

When speaking from a conception perspective, a woman will always know the feeling of nurturing her baby boy from day one. However, her instincts will alert her to the differences between a man and a baby boy, unless the man fights her nurturing instincts and confuses them with control, leaving him scarred!

"LEARN TO SHED OLD SKIN AND ALLOW
NEW FLESH TO GROW. REMEMBER THE
THINGS THAT CAUSED YOUR PAIN—
THAT OPEN WOUND. THE WOUNDS OF
LYING, DECEIVING, HURTING, CHEATING,
AND ABUSE WILL GO AWAY ONCE YOUR
WOUND IS HEALED CORRECTLY, AND
NOT COVERED WITH A SCAB BUT WITH
NEW FLESH!"

~ LEON R. WALKER JR~

THAT SCAR

Baby, I know who you are,

in the dark as well as in the light, that's our scar.

No, no, oh no, don't cover it up, that's our scar.

That's our bundle of joy, our baby boy, our baby girl.

You know, Cheryl, named after you, after you,

you after your mother, another Cheryl.

Would I change it? Never in this world.

See, that scar, I was a part of that.

No, don't cover it with a tat, our scar.

We planned that scar, we rub that scar.

We see that scar, we feel that scar. To me,

it's not a scar, it's who we are,

a family, waiting to be, wanting to be,

all that we, planned to be,

graciously, damned to be,

away from me.

Oh Lord, I cry to you,

patiently, that scar to be

there forever, as a reminder to me.

When you came to me, rubbing c—c —c section,

worried about my rejection,

never will I deny the home of which she

was delivered to me, he was delivered to me,

making me a father to be,

a caring husband of three.

The only pain that I see,

is when you think that scar bothers me.

That's our scar baby.

Let's Talk – A lot of times, women cover themselves up, shower alone, get dressed in the dark, and turn away when with a man who is either clothed or not. How often they forget that the beauty of giving birth is an emotional, heart-wrenching, love-growing time in your life, but you tend to leave that part out after it's all over. Once you give birth, you begin to, of course, love your child, but what most women do is to start to worry about how he'll look at you, if he still loves you, and if he'll still feel the same about you sexually. Of course, your body has changed, but as men, it's our job to keep you confident despite what your body just went through. We don't do that enough, if hardly at all. We have to love you even more from that point forward. It's not a task, as most start to feel that way; it's now our way of life. It's ours, all of it.

PEARLS

- Stop blaming your past and get past your blames

- There's a difference between taking and receiving. When a person receives from you, they do so from a great source and are more inclined to give back, in any way. When they take, it's for their own selfish reasons and they do not intend to return the favor. Receiving is pure and touches the heart! Give and take has been explained wrong for many years.

- Sometimes—-we're just not ready for ourselves. You have to make us believe and know who we are.

- You have to be ok with not being right.

- Wash one another down while in the shower, and then lotion each other.

- She'll give you many ways out, before she commits.

- Men and hardened women cry on the inside—therefore, we die on the inside. When we remain closed off, you'll only see our pain in my eyes and not hear it.

- Sometimes we find happiness by being unhappy for just a little while—even finding the right person during unhappy times. When you're a genuine person, and you're unhappy, a genuine person will notice it and find you.

- When men don't talk, women hurt.

- You'll know when you're too good for a person, their reciprocity will not exist. These types of people are called EAP's, Empty Ass People! They're obvious very early on.

THE FORGOTTEN KISS

You don't even kiss,
you think just because you have size, you can skip the kiss,
my kiss. You want this, you better learn how to kiss.
His lips are dry; I have gloss, you need gloss.
You act like you don't know what I want, that kiss,
that kiss, an art that's lost, crusty.
Don't touch me, his lips are crusty.
Where did the intimacy go? You see, intimacy, crazy, like me,
asking for a kiss, he can't see,
with that size, and a wonderful kiss, he can have me, grab me,
force me, lead me, kiss me, take me away, bliss me.
I haven't been kissed, it's been such a long time, it's not even missed.
His thoughts go straight to my pants, you know, the gist of it all.
He was never taught to kiss, to take his time,
to find the line, that line,
when my lips are closed,
waiting for that kiss, that kiss, my mind explodes.
He knows me, see that line, a fine line, a fine face,
that place, my mouth, not down south, not yet.
He has to learn to get things right,
like face-to-face, lips aligned, drinking wine, my mouth opens for
that wine.
His mouth should be that smooth, soft wine, wine,
wine that I can't resist, wish it was him, him, wish it was that kiss.
Slow, yeah, slow, passionate, slow, breathe with me,
be with me, into me, please kiss me.
I will breathe into he, he into me,
continuously, as we weep together, we pass life between these,
waiting lips taking sips, that wine,
damn, damn, damn, that wine opened my mouth,
not him, he went too fast, trying to go down south.
No, up here, up here, up here, come closer,
please, kiss my mouth.

Let's Talk—I've heard women say, "Well, it's been so long, I've forgotten how to kiss." Unfortunately, I learned how to kiss in the first grade, with my cousins. As sick as that sounds, they did teach me. To this day, I think they gave me a good lesson, albeit an inappropriate one. I don't care who you are or what you say or how often you complain about kissing, one thing is for sure; once you're kissed good and passionately, your opinions on kissing change instantly. Most women have men who either don't know how or don't like to kiss. You allow that to happen, going years without being kissed.

Some women say that kissing is too personal; I agree and disagree. I suppose it is personal, since I love it so much, but I have a hard time turning down a kiss, honestly. I know women who will have sex with a man but won't kiss him; they turn their heads away when the man tries to kiss them. I met someone like that too, until I grabbed her face gently, turned her mouth towards mine, and kissed her. I believe, at that time, me forcing a kiss on her was a turn on; it surely made it more intense for me. She did, however, kiss me back, and the second time, she grabbed my face. I like to kiss like it's the last time, seriously. Lips are not the only thing to kiss and I'm not referring to your vagina either.

Areas of need are, but not limited to:

Her knuckles, fingers, knees, the back of her legs, neck, forehead, forearms, ears, shoulders, back (all over), butt cheeks, toes, elbows, and under her breast. Men skip a lot of these places and go right to her vagina; that's a huge mistake.

Another technique that I learned is this: We'll lie side by side, hugging closely, then I'll breathe slowly together with her while my mouth meets hers. I inhale her breath and she inhales mine. We're in unison, no tongue movements, just enjoying each other's breath! I call this *Giving Life.*

Lesson Twenty-eight: Stop being bossy

There's' nothing sexy or cool about being bossy! In fact, it severely damages your personality. A lot of men lose interested in many things, when you're bossy. What's worse is that, you'll dare to allow him to boss you around, yet, the kids and your boss will do it to you, and you'll accept it. You will not only ruin your partner, but you will also stunt their relationship growth, by being bossy! When you're bossy, expect to be shut out of many things, for one, communication. I highly suggest that you use that energy being bossy, to call on your partner about how he or she feels about your bossy ways. It's a hard and painful question to ask, and there will be even more pain from what you may hear. Don't be surprised if your kids feel the same way! That single, unhappy, scorned girlfriend that you brag to, about your partner's inadequacies, well she's rooting for your marriage to fail and you'll never know. Most likely, she doesn't sleep with you, eat with you, or live with you. Her recommendations, comments, or compliments are based on what you want to hear, only.

As your friend hangs up the phone...

"Honey, you won't believe what Lisa just told me about her husband..."

You may notice that, she never tells you *anything* about her husband, wife, or family issues. A few key things that are signs of a partner becoming tired of you being bossy;

- Acting like they've forgotten to do something, anything. At this point, they really don't care anymore.
- Other things interest them, more than you.
- Hours, or even days without talking or texting, while you're out of town.
- Eagerness to pay for your trips away.
- Their vehicle is clean, but not yours.

You can correct this, though. This also goes for bossy men, too. You must start to correct your deficiencies, right after asking him/her how they feel. Never go back on your word. You can't be afraid of losing power, it's about gaining your partner back, most of whom haven't had any power, for sometime, so they don't even recognize it. Practicing the act of giving in, and your partner will grow in...in love with you again!

MILK

I love you, this is for you, my milk.

Warm, nurturing, nourishing, my milk, like silk,

made from me, through God you see, he gave me

this milk to help you grow, learn, take life from me.

Yes, my milk, it has to be, only from me. I am your mother, eternally,

internally you started to flee my ovary,

captured to grow from me, producing was free.

Your milk, my body, my soul, yeah, I taste it from me.

It's yours, for free, cautiously, oozing crazily,

into your soul, grow for me, my milk, my milk.

I made this milk, just for you, you made this milk,

just for me. My baby is going to see.

The bond that we create powerfully,

will not be broken.

It's poetry, yes, it's spoken,

into your life, into your life,

can't wait to be, can't wait to see.

You develop for me, all from my ability to give you this wonderful,

powerful, breast formula, nature seed, righteous feed.

No one can be close to me, over me, right by me,

by me.

Bye, I need to breast-feed!

Let's talk- From the onset, breast-feeding is the early stage of nurturing for little boys. What we often forget, or are ashamed of is learning from what breast-feeding develops into. There's an invaluable, impenetrable, and untouchable connection that transpires here. When a child is in the "hunger" stage, the mind rapidly connects to survival mode of and from the mother, to be fed! Well--so does the feeling of hunger, so persist for and in a man. This stage is feeding our *need* for reassuring confidence, comfort, and fulfillment. Our pursuit of continued affection, and guidance transitions from her breast, to her mind, from her mind, to our mind, and then into our heart--from *breast-feeding, to chest-feeding!*

TOUCH MYSELF

I touch myself, watch myself, love myself,

I am into me, without you, I am into me, with you, I am into myself.

You put me last, I put me first, I touch myself.

I was me without you, you are not you without me, I touch myself

so amazingly. Gratification, stimulation, I touch myself,

by myself, learning myself, I touch myself.

Self... touch... I... gives me, me, gives me, freedom, freedom from

your touch,

no clutch is such that I need your touch that much.

I have more than you can offer; strong, sound, morally fit, spiritu-

ally legit,

I have more than you can offer. I'm not easy, I won't settle.

I'm a woman, I can keep up. I, too, have wit.

Can you, do you, are you? Those are my questions,

lessons, blessings, my touch is fierce, too much for you, another question.

It's been years, since...your touch,

no more will I crave what's... so natural, cause, I touch,

I touch, faithfully, yeah. I touch myself,

you think it's monogamy, but you see, it's three,

ménage a trois; you, me,

and my mind, I touch myself mentally!

Let's Talk — Women are generally emotionally ahead of some men because they are more in tune with their hearts, minds, and souls—their *Sensual Circuitry*—before anything or anywhere else. They become excited to learn themselves, but more importantly, they can't wait to share their newfound discovery with a man or woman. It's a different touch, which gives them mental stimulation.

BODY PORTIONS—ages 25 and up!
Visual images transferred to a woman's sensory perception will get her ready before you kiss anywhere. She'll get her mind ready for you to take her to higher levels of intimacy. Just don't blow it! Some women, if not all, look at the lips before looking at a man's penis print. This prepares their mind and body before anything happens.

Men with full lips can be gentler. At the sight of full lips, a woman sets her mind in motion for "soft & plump." Words transferred to her sensory perception will get her ready before you kiss her body anywhere, hence the phrase "Soft & Plump." She'll get her mind ready for you to take her to higher levels of intimacy. Don't blow it!

Men with small and tight lips can get a tighter grip on body parts and can make the pleasure more intense. Some women look at the lips right before or right after looking at a man's penis print. This prepares their mind and body before anything happens. I've dated women with both types of lips, so I know how each type feels.

Here are some erogenous body portions you can explore to spice up your romance:

Body Portion #1 - **The back of her neck**
Gently kiss her, either at the top or base of her neck (where her back starts). It really doesn't matter where. The nerve endings are connected to her lower spine and the tingle will spread all the way down.

Stand behind her and gently push her hair upwards. Begin to kiss her there, in the middle of the neck and on the jugulars, and she'll surely lose her footing. It's a slow melt for her, so you must hold and support her gently. The more you kiss this area, the more she'll want to give into and please you.

Suck and lick down her neck and across both shoulders and back, making sure that each time, you go right back up to the top of her neck. Once at the top, take turns kissing each jugular again, giving her tender, suction-like kisses, while keeping your mouth warm. Next, softly and passionately slide your tongue and lips down to the bottom of her neck, in a slow sucking motion. Gently suck that area as well.

The entire time, you must do six things:

i. Control her head movement by placing your clean, pleasant-smelling hands (use cologne or lotion), under her chin to turn her head opposite of the side you are kissing her on. This slightly stretches her skin (on the kissed side) and makes it even more sensitive. Tell her what to do, she'll follow along,

ii. Gently press your tongue into the middle (back) of her neck. Caress her bare breast with your warm hands.

iii. Slowly grind on her from behind and pull her close so that you can whisper softly in her ear about how good she smells!

iv. After about twenty *good, slow, and passionate* minutes (you must not rush), unbuckle her pants and slowly unzip them (if she hasn't done so already). Gently rub her clitoris by gliding and moving with her. Be sure to keep your nails out of the way and trim them—it will be quite slippery!

v. Spread her natural lube on her vaginal lips.

vi. While spreading her sweet honey (by now it should be on her thighs too), make sure it flows evenly. Use either of your legs to slowly open her legs, then remove your hand and share the tasteful delight, together. As you insert your honey-filled finger in her mouth, kiss her. When you're with a woman who hasn't tasted herself (believe me, there are some) as a man, you must talk to her about it, saying: "See, baby, this is what you taste like. Doesn't it taste good?"

Here are some phrases to use while taking care of her neck and shoulders:

- Damn, baby, you smell good.
- Wow, you are delicious!
- I couldn't wait for you to come home.
- Can you feel my heartbeat?
- I want you so bad.
- I admire you
- Oh God!

Body Portion #2 - **The "G-spot"**
Don't be in a hurry to just "stick it in." Her G-spot is very sensual and sensitive. Gay women are particularly good at finding the G-spot. It's very easy to find—about an inch inside of her vaginal walls, upwards, towards her pelvic area. You can find it by inserting your middle finger or both the middle and index finger slowly (ensure your nails are manicured), along with some lubrication. It's a small, ribbed area where everything else inside of her feels smooth, so you'll feel a difference when you touch it. I highly suggested that you do this AFTER she's turned on so that you can use her natural lubrication.

Kissing, rubbing, and caressing her breast along with some mental stim-ulation will also help tremendously. Also, discuss stimulating her G-spot beforehand, in great detail. Some women have already felt this sensation and might feel like they have to urinate. That's all true, but you must tell her to relax when she feels this way. Their mind quickly wants to run to the toilet. She doesn't really have to urinate; it's her mind that thinks she does. If she's turned on enough, she'll want you to continue gently stroking her spot. The G-spot area will slowly swell with fluids—IT IS NOT URINE!

Kiss her deeply and slowly. Keep her legs spread open while she's on her back. As you feel her wetness start to flow and she begins to moan (because she will) and breathes deeply, add more light pressure, on her G-spot, rubbing in a "come here" motion with one or two fingers.

For some women, it may take some time, so be patient. However, for others, their juices will begin to flow quickly. Slow the strokes down as she gets wetter and push upwards more. This will cause the fluid to flow with each stroke of your finger. Keep her mind there, with sensual and sexual words or conversation, but not so much that it takes her mind off the feeling that she's beginning to enjoy.

Body Portion #3 - **The Wrist**
The wrist is an area that has been neglected for years. I found this area by accident when I was being goofy. Kiss around it and bite it softly, too. Occasionally, gently pin her arms down with both your hands and just take your time exploring it. Kiss the wrist a few times in a circular motion. Watch her legs as they slowly move around. She'll even look at you while you do this. Sometimes, she'll look away in amazement. However, on most occasions, your lady will caress her own breasts! Sex should never start in the bedroom!

After or during the circular kiss, take your lips off slightly, keeping them about an inch away—just breathing on her wrist.

Enjoy!

Body Portion #4 - **The Lower Back**

The lower back is so close to her sensitive butt-cheeks that the tingling sensation goes right to each of her butt-cheeks. You must grip her hips tightly to move her around, slow her down when she squirms, because she will.

She won't mind relinquishing control because it feels much better for her to let go while you take over her lower back and anxious butt-cheeks. Reach your hands around to her upper thighs and massage them while you kiss her lower back, across the entire area. It's also very sensual to her when you place your chest down on her butt during the entire time. Body contact is always very important to women; they enjoy feeling not only your body heat but your heartbeat, too!

Shifting upwards while you lay on her butt-cheeks, massage her thighs and kiss her lower back. Whisper to her (don't ask) to raise herself up and gently hold her beast in the palms of your hands while you continue passionately kissing and licking her lower back.

Body Portion #5 - **Inside of Her Butt-Cheeks**

Lay her on her stomach so she's nice and comfortable. This inside of her buttocks is *very, very* sensitive. Lick both of them; don't ever neglect either one! It's important not to spread them apart, as this reduces the sensitivity, so just let her lay natural. When you're ready, open them slightly by slightly pulling each one, making sure to gently massage them. As you continue to devour her cheeks, increase the pressure of the massages. The massages add extra delight.

While concentrating on one side, you must use the palm of your other hand to give her a slow and deep massage on the other cheek, too. Gentle kisses and occasionally sucking on them makes the feeling more intense! She'll let you know when she's ready to make love because, at this point, it won't be sex! Your woman will really appreciate it if you do this because most men won't go down there.

Body Portion #6 - **Behind Her Knees**
You can kiss this area a little roughly, preferably just slightly rough; not too gently either as this will tickle her, which we don't want.

Body Portion #7 - **On Her Knee Caps**
Have her lie down. Ensure her knees are relaxed and straight—this will give her more pleasure. Kiss the sides and bottom of the knee, *not on* the kneecap itself.

Body Portion #8 - **Under Her Breast**
Most men aim right for the nipple, or on the sides. While this is good, getting a little more creative and adventurous won't hurt. Suck gently on the underside of her breast. She'll want to caress her own breasts but don't let her; this will drive her crazy.

Ask her to put her hands behind her head and leave them right there while laying down. To make things even spicier, demand that she watch you as you do this while grinding her pelvic area on your body.

Body Portion #9 – **Top of Her Breast**
Sit up while she lays down. Kiss the top of her chest, not her breast—right beneath the collar bone. She'll rub the hell out of your back while you are on top of her. She'll want to pull you down onto her. Support yourself while leaning over her. Do not touch or kiss anywhere else except the top of her breast.

Body Portion #10 - **The Outside of Her Hands and Arms**
Lick and kiss the entire outside of her hands and arm, all the way up to her elbow. Just because.

Body Portion #11 - **Her Elbow**
Suck directly on her elbow, on it, and inside it. That's all.

Body Portion #12 - **Her Fingers**
Lick between her fingers.

Body Portion #13 - **Her Palm**
Suck and bite the *thick part* of her lower thumb, near the palm area

Body Portion #14 - **Her Lower Bicep**
Suck and bite gently the area where the lower part of her bicep starts.

Body Portion #15 - **The Inside of Her Hands**
Lick this entire part; spend more time at the base of her thumb.

Body Portion #16 - **The Pinky**
I think this is the most sensitive finger. Suck and nibble on it gently. While sucking your way up to the knuckle, swirl your tongue around it. Take it all the way in your mouth and look at her. After a few minutes, remove her finger, and replace it with your finger in her mouth, then kiss her!

Body Portion #17 - **Her Forehead**
Kiss her forehead all the way across. Throw in a gentle suck each time, then stop on her cheekbones and suck there too.

Body Portion #18 - **Her Chin**
Suck on it.

Body Portion #19 - **Her Teeth**
Run your tongue across her teeth.

Body Portion #20 - **Bottom Lip and Tongue**

Suck lightly on both while you kiss her

Body Portion #21 - **Chest to Back**
While she's lying on her stomach in bed, spread her legs with yours and just lay on top of her; your arms along hers, your chest against her back, and your face behind her head, as she faces away from you. Her turning her face away from yours is to ensure comfort. As long as you are on top of her, she'll think of you, if she's happy. Next, slowly put your hands over hers and intertwine your fingers, keeping your member lying right on her vaginal area, no penetration—for now. Lie there naked but rotate every now and then, staying behind her for ease of breathing and comfort. Make sure to cup her breasts as you shift positions from being on top to laying behind her, and wrapping your legs around hers.

Body and Mind Portion #22 - **Explore**
Explore your own body to enjoin your partner to discover the same things that you like, love, and especially desire. Knowing what you desire will bring fire! Teach them things that will give both of you wings. The sex will soar, and you will not be sore!

Be honest about being honest. If you're not honest, be honest about not being honest, that's just as powerful and liberating.

Body Portion #23 - **The Clitoris**
Like I mentioned in the Pearls section, learning how to please a woman's clit speaks—in great detail —to gay women! Sometimes, the gay woman has learned about her own clitoris from an older gay woman.

Body Portion #24 - **The Inner Thighs**
Her inner thighs. Take your time and suck and kiss these areas. Please, do not rush to sex; allow her to enjoy it. It's quite fun to start at the ankles and go up! Be sure to stop at the inner knee area, too. Once you get to her upper

thigh area, right where the thigh and lower abdomen connect, you'll see a crease. That area, up to her hip bone, is prime real estate. She'll not only want to move and getaway, but she'll also admire the fact that you have found a new area for the two of you.

Body Portion #25 - **The Nipples**

Her nipples are very sensitive or might desire a nice, tight, suction on them, depending on the size. Don't be afraid to ask her what she likes, it's ok. Run your tongue around the entire areola, slowly! Some women like to feel a coldness on their nipples while some like nipple clips, but they all like a warm, gentle mouth with succulent kisses in between.

This is the end of "Body Portions," but there are more erogenous zones on her body to discover. As a couple, you must explore each other's body to find out what they like but haven't found. It's much more special when you're in a committed relationship—it keeps the relationship very spicy. Body Portions is mainly about learning about one another and not always about sex. However, it will lead to that. Sometimes you just need to have edible fun!

Chapter Twenty Eight

Toys and Accessories

There are two important and crucial things to remember. Firstly, it's not always about "toys." As a man, I totally missed the point here. I was first intimidated by the notion of my woman wanting anything else other than what I could provide in the bedroom.

Secondly, being open, trusting, showing a willingness to explore more of her body, and confidence in your abilities to satisfy her takes precedence over everything else, *size* included. Women are more inclined to want emotional satisfaction, above all. Like I mentioned earlier in the book, an endowed man who's not aware of her erogenous zones will always bypass her most sensitive nerve endings, not to mention skipping foreplay!

To some women, size is important because their first encounter was with a well-endowed man, giving them a false sense of what good sex is. She has not experienced a more sensual level of sex, or more importantly, love-making. To most, size plays a small (no pun intended) role in satisfaction. What women see first can and will affect her decision to move forward with a guy that doesn't possess the size she thinks she desires. However, a man who pays attention to her body language and isn't selfish when sex begins, one who knows what he's doing will ultimately win her over! Don't be selfish—your job is to get her to orgasm first!

Another important thing about toys or accessories is that having conversations about sexual activities in the bedroom is just as important as the toys themselves. Sometimes it takes a man a little time to get his ego in check, but you should never be afraid to have toys in the bedroom.

I know some of you, both men and women, don't want or will not allow toys in the bedroom. Some men might become offended, but you shouldn't.

Women like variety and it's especially important that you oblige. Rejection is not an option here—this is her time to lead you. Allowing her gives her a feeling of importance and makes her want to try new things. Above all, it shows your woman that you trust her!

There's nothing like being deep in sleep and all of a sudden, you hear the Rabbit or Bullet vibrating because you left her hanging. It's also a good idea for you to shop for toys and recommend some to her. This is something you should talk about, sooner or later.

You don't always have to buy vibrators. You could buy candle wax too. However, make sure the area you plan to use the wax on has a coat of oil. The oil adds a layer of protection just in case the wax is too hot. Nipple clips are sensual as well. The motion lotion works well—just don't use too much, and get a nice flavor you both like. Buy some plastic sheets and oil each other down so that you're very slippery and warm!

Body painting is fun too. Buy the fluorescent kind and have *fun with words* on each other's bodies. You can make it a guessing game. There are two reasons why body painting is great. One, writing sexual words can be fun. Secondly, and more importantly, his/her finger writing on you is pleasurable in itself—happy writing!

PEARLS

- When you go backwards, all you'll get is back-words.

- Liars plan to lie and lie to plan.

- An apology has to accompany a hug, eye contact, maybe even a gift, or a dinner date. If not, then you're just saying it without any meaning or substance. Do not repeat the apology, when this happens, either you don't believe it yourself, you have childhood fears, the victim wasn't receptive, or your misstep is repeated behavior. Make it meaningful and not repetitive.

- Remember to discuss menopause when she's ready. it's a must. Help her feel balanced during this time and do not make fun of her hot flashes.

- Are you a disciplinarian or dictatornarian? As either, you tend to *run* the household. You may feel that this is necessary, but I don't feel that way. If we disagree, that's fine, but please allow me to caution you. Just like iron fist leaders in companies or corporate america, they experience high turnover ratios and low morale! Do you want that in your house? Leon, how can I have a high turnover ratio in my house? Well, by the husband, wife, or kids *turning over* a good attitude, to a bad attitude because you feel like you have to run your household with an iron fist. As strict disciplinarians, you won't be alone but you will be lonely. Kids and spouses will share secrets, anger, and many other things about you, with one another and you will not know, and your house will feel cold! For the ***dictatornarian.*** it'll take you two to three relationships before you get it and learn why you push everyone away. Notice, I stated house and not home, there's a difference.

Chapter Twenty Nine

The Types

In this chapter, I will discuss different "types" of women and men in relationships. Some of these types of people you may likely have encountered or will encounter in a relationship. They include the following:

The Unconditional-Dimensional

If she keeps asking you how she looks, if the sex is good, etc., it is because she has been deeply hurt, offended, and lied to. A lot of times, the hurt and pain come from her own family. I've seen this happen when women are disowned by their families for dating outside of their race. The family has made it known that they think she's filthy and hearing this can hurt deeply! There's a good chance that she has biracial kids too.

She's not completely one-dimensional, but her strong traits are too tough for her family and some men to handle, so she focuses on what she wants to hear from her man. The men might consider her pushy or needy—she's not. She's fair, genuine, loving, thoughtful, and deeply caring. Her first dimension is to seek validation; she does this because she wants to improve herself for you and no one else. This woman can and will be faithful. She's smart, worldly, driven, passionate, and compassionate, and a lot of men miss out on her.

The Single for Years

This type is usually waiting for a long-time ex, one who is either married now or scarred for what seems like a lifetime. She harbors years of regret because, during her growing stages, she was afraid to open up. Her morals were deep, so she didn't allow him to come to her calling—it was too silent! This woman is really reserved, neat, clean, and guarded— but not that open.

She'll never get over her ex, who was a soul-mate that she found early in life. She tries hard with other men not to have the chemistry she had with the old ex. Her next relationship will be mediocre, at best. If this is you, stop having low self-esteem and desiring a relationship so bad, that it shows on your face and is heard through your conversation.

Don't make it a priority to date and meet a man, let him come to you. Apply yourself into understanding what you lost, in order not to repeat the mistake. You want to know why these men come and go. Is it you or is it them? Opening up and understanding what you lost, in addition to your inner beauty will bring you the right man. Be patient because the older you get, the more agitated you'll become with the small things, thus changing the axis of your energy.

You will exude both positive and negative energies, depending on who you meet, so manage both well. It will also help you radiate confidence instead of hope and desperation— making a spiritual connection easy to make! You have awesome qualities but haven't given yourself a chance to explore like-minded people because your first love was a great guy with whom you had a strong connection.

The Fearful

This type is afraid to move forward because of the damage wreaked by their ex. A lot of times, this becomes an excuse to just date forever. People are really damaged from past relationships, however, it's disrespectful to carry that into your current relationship. You're almost comparing them to the last person. Give yourself a chance by giving a different person a chance to know and help you grow. Stop being afraid, you're grown now.

Cancel the rental application you approved to let your ex live in your head! Sometimes, we have the best people in our corner and don't realize it because their own kids become our distraction. Please remember that just because you're not their biological parent doesn't mean that they won't take to your teachings. Some people are donors while others are just carriers—don't discard that.

Kids can and should be shared. We weren't perfect kids; not by far! Sometimes, raising someone else's children helps you realize that you didn't do so well with your own kids. When people let you into their children's life, they're looking for a better parent for their kids. Keep that in mind and go back to implement, with your own kids, what you have learned in the new relationship. If you don't see a difference, you're not making a difference. Be honored and not Ornery!

The 'Mine, Not Yours'

"Take care of my kids, but not yours." I have seen women do this a lot and it's not fair. Believe me, there will come a time when your own kids will not be taken care of anymore. You either do it together or end it. Kids are forever, good or bad; they're not going away, so be fair! You may think your partner is happy, but trust me, they probably have a confidant and work overtime just to stay away from home.

The Celebrity Chaser

Known all over the world, gets old really fast and her looks fade too. She will never be right for a man because her morals are off. She will, more than likely, end up alone. However, if she does get married or gets in a relationship without fixing herself, she'll crave the limelight once again. Her conversations are only centered on her past. These women usually have to deal with the karma of home-wrecking, sooner or later.

The Player

Has body odor and hasn't broken ties with their soul ties from years back. Most times, this person is stuck in the past and will never grow up. Can only talk about their past, just like the Celebrity Chaser; they know each other well. Usually has a nice car and stays at home with mom, waiting to inherit her house and bank account

The Rich Homemaker

Your life has passed you by, or so you think. This is when the internal torture starts. You have forgotten about yourself and cry yourself to sleep and also cry to your friends. You start to become a recluse due to embarrassment.

There were nice trips, a nice house, cars, and all of the best jewelry. Years later, hubby now travels alone, golfing and jet setting, leaving you at home by yourself. Your kids are grown and the role of "grandma" is creeping up on you. You still get horny but there's no one around, so you binge on Netflix, the Lifetime shows, and your vibrator, trying to keep your sanity. The times have gone by all too fast and the "cougar" is written all over you—you're extremely lonely.

Your imagination runs wild. You constantly think about "what if" and "how did I get this way" but you will not cheat, although you fantasize about various men. You are married but now, only to your morals! Later, you file for divorce, claiming emotional neglect, and get everything, including your boy toy yet you are still unhappy. You haven't been wealthy in years, and haven't had a man make love to you. You begin to feel worthless and doubt runs deep, with you wondering "will I die alone and lonely?"

However, this situation can change. Men that live this way ultimately meet and date younger women but these men get old, quick. You, the Rich Homemaker, will regain your youth by simply not giving up. I highly suggest getting into groups of successful, like-minded women who can share their similar stories and how they overcome then and are now enjoying life. After doing so, you'll come to realize that of all the nice things you had, all the riches were, for the most part, shared with you at a much younger and impressionable age. They didn't mean anything and nothing was ever bought in your name. Now, you're happier with the small things, your mind, youth, and dignity. More importantly, you'll see that you were sucked in just like the newer young ladies!

The Toughie

The tough girl who grew up amongst boys and men. She is more in touch with her masculine side but loves men, regardless. She doesn't like flowers, she's not mushy but does desire sex. Pretty easy to get along with but struggles to be feminine. She will not get too emotional but has deep feelings. Wants or needs a man every now and then, but he's not a "must-have" for her. She yearns to be treated like a lady but she cannot rid herself of her attraction to the "rough-house men." You'll find the innocent, nice, and loving young lady in you when you realize that you miss being a woman, a side of you that you can summon when you want to because she's within you.

The Cheated On

This woman will always wonder "what's wrong with me?" You want a relationship but it has come to a point where you've all but given up. They say opposites attract but there must come a time when you find a man who's very similar to you, morally. That's your safe haven; more likely than not, that man has been cheated on too. You have all of the great qualities but are stuck in a world full of immoral people and you spend too much time asking "why" instead of knowing "how!" You are attracted to the wrong man, this will lead you to a "Relationship Mismatch" This woman has always given the benefit of doubt. Next time, follow your doubt and leave out the benefit!

If you go into a relationship that's based on sex and physical appearances, you have already failed. Most good-looking and sexually active people rely solely on their looks and sexual prowess. This relationship is emotionally based and motivated; it works only when you're thinking of sex, engaged in sex, or are promiscuous.

After all is said and done, the feelings that you go into the sexual relationship with, disappear after an orgasm! There were never any true or deep emotional feelings or plans to move forward into a relationship, but one person lied and the other never said anything.

Most times, after being hurt, some women start to enjoy one-night-stands because they miss the companionship and still desire a relationship. They will then settle for what the man wants— about a good hour of sex, no cuddling, and no hugging.

Regardless, the woman will intuitively think or want a relationship built-in "one night" without discussing future plans, and will end up heartbroken, misled, and left standing for many nights with oneself, over and over again—even while being married!

The Professional Athlete

Has been given everything—*except the truth*. This renders them incapable of dealing with many things when they reach the highest level. The sport doesn't matter because once they become icons, start making money, receive television and book deals, the plastic, money-hungry, fake-ass people come out. Their only agenda is to take and make money off of these athletes. For many years, they've lived their lives without knowing most people around them.

Some of them are even being forced to play their sport: cheerleading, rodeo, ice skating, tennis, snowboarding, hockey and many more, because their parents want to live vicariously through their children. All along, the parents see dollar signs and not the signs of people with only greed in their hearts and soul. Some so-called growth experts, i.e. parents and agents even consult with doctors at an early age about a child that might or might not be theirs. They focus on the child's growth potential—physically and not mentally. This is the first inclination to not only greed but misguidance—away from reality, proper grooming, and the development of important life skills. By the time the young man or woman reaches the proverbial "praised height and weight" pipe dream they've been put on, it's nothing more than a pedestal built from the claws and dirty hands of greedy, envious, human-trafficking *demons!*

The child won't have true friends nor will they truly know their own parents. They have better relationships with their coaches and agents than anyone—people who don't share their true-life experiences, encounters, genetics, or DNA with. They have nothing in common except for their pockets and contracts! Nonetheless, there are some coaches and agents who are truly genuine but there are not many of them.

The professional athletes will be lied to by men and women looking for sex, the spotlight, money, a child, and a lawsuit. There are people in this world who like to kiss ass and some who like their asses kissed. This is a collision course that will happen either sooner or later.

Women aren't the only groupies—there are male groupies too. They become just as jealous as women. Most of these athletes have never been groomed to be "Grooms or or built to be, Brides," therefore, they have no clue about leading themselves into healthy relationships or marriages. Most of them just want to be brought down gently to earth, by honest people. The very tall female athlete—sure, she wants a man her height—will at some point, love, date, and even marry a genuine man or woman who's much shorter than she is; one who makes her feel normal again. Their hearts have never been filled and they have many voids! As these athletes grow older, the money, fame, and fanfare start to wear off, fast. It becomes a distant memory, even for the coach who propositioned or touched them! A lot of them who have been touched, coerced, or blackmailed will have a tough time transitioning away from the sport which they loved, into a healthy relationship. However, it can be done by surrounding yourself with people that genuinely care for your life and future, not your money, connections, or network/net worth.

What most of them are missing is a *true mentor,* one that's mature, aware, has character and integrity. I have a couple of friends who coach millionaire athletes and CEOs and what I have noticed is that these millionaire men and women are regular people that hurt, cry, have doubt, become weak, addicted, but most importantly, they just want to be around people who care about their livelihood and health, not their wealth. They'll be surprised by what people offer them, after years of selling their souls to the people that offered them the same thing.

Once you become drafted in any sport, your "abuse" credentials (financial, sexual, and spiritual) skyrocket. For the top draft picks, basically all first-rounders, you become financially sexy to the devil's tentacles, and they come in all races, ages, height, and weight. You'll not only take care of that person, but you'll also pay his or her mortgage, cell phone bills, family trips, and daycare for their children. Once you get injured, they have no problem forgetting about you. For many years, these athletes have missed genuine help, haven't smiled, can't hold a decent conversation about life, don't know how to manage their money, can't run a household, and many start to deal with childhood issues. Sadly, most of these athletes leave behind real friends and do more for people they barely know. You become indebted to them, fast and for a long time. We all know how it goes:

"Damn, baby, you're fine, sexy as hell. I think I love you. I wanna be with you."

Or

"I think you're hot. You look good tonight. You're beautiful, you got a man?"

We have no idea what this person is like on the inside or who they really are. All we really know is that they're wealthy, but just because a person is wealthy doesn't mean that they're well!

The Giver

Consistently gives from their soul. Will always wind up hurt because their first instinct is to make their partner happy, even when the other person only wants temporary and instant gratification. There's only a beginning in sight, no end—only an end for what they want to take from you, if it does end! The giver must begin to practice patience to find the person that's also a giver as well. More often than not, it'll be a person that's also been hurt and taken advantage of, and the two of you know that pain all too well.

When you meet someone like this, you'll know because they are patient, hesitant, and sometimes, apprehensive. Pay attention to how they act or react while in your company because most times, you'll find yourself in them. If you laugh, apologize, and explain why you chuckled, laughed, or preferably, smiled—it'll make them much more comfortable. More importantly, they'll realize that there are other givers just like them. A taker will first exude their inability to give. They'll do this by ignoring a bill while at dinner, they won't plan anything or have any ideas, and they'll wait for you to do everything. It is possible to meet like-minded and heart-minded people, but you *must* exercise control over your emotions through your sensory perception. Givers are very insightful.

Givers are quick to make things, situations, and people better at any cost, therefore, they are very impulsive and wear their feelings and emotions on their sleeves, thus becoming very obvious. Givers also pay attention to the other person's wants, needs, and desires in every little detail. Givers are great managers of resources and time and are well kept themselves. When they keep things, they do it for others and not for themselves. You'll know the takers right away because those people will accept any and everything immediately. They'll sit back and let you do everything, without reaching in their own pocket, picking up the phone to text or call, or even giving you a compliment. You give because this is your *highest point of energy*, whether you get hurt or not. Sometimes you over do it, simply take that as a sign and remain aware. Takers will take in everything, but mostly what's beneficial to them, if it's not beneficial, their dissatisfaction will show, they cant hide it. Most, if not all, are ungrateful. Most givers become lost in their extending services, why? Well it's because you're a very loving person, exhausting yourself to unloving, unappreciative, people! Givers always fill up, but end up with an empty tank!

The Goer-Back and Forth-er

The Goer-Back- and Forth-er will give, just like the giver, but wants the same thing in return and will hold that desire against you. These types of people have been through a lot and don't like to waste time or have their time wasted. Some have been abused, disrespected, and hurt or didn't have much of a voice in their previous relationship, and now not only refuse to back down but also shut-up!

In their "new" life, they vow to never be treated that way again, yet will on occasion, treat the new person like this. They don't realize that they've spent many years with a sick or addicted person, and they've taken on some of the addicted person's ways; they even sound like them! *The Goer-Back and Forth-er* is naturally sweet and caring but their reputation for anger precedes them in most cases, and they've become bitter about many things. When conversing with this man or woman, they'll tend to repeat the issues about their past and will also over-talk you. Their hurt runs deep. Conversations can be good, but will most likely be one-sided, long-winded, all the while dominating it, thus always repelling people.

In a lot of cases, their trust has dwindled as well. This type will tend to believe, think, and feel that what they say is truth and law. Also, when they respond to a text or email, they'll take their time to properly construct it, giving it tons of energy, both negative and positive, but always ending on a negative note. I must admit, though. They are good husbands and wives.

The Easy-Pleasing Woman

A very dangerous woman to most men. For the woman, she'll accept almost anything; coming over late, seeing other women, leaving her in the middle of the night, texting other women while you're with her, and on some occasions, she'll consider having another woman in the bedroom. She accepts this because she does it too, and doesn't expect much in return. Just be fair—she's ok with being in this dirty game and plays it well. She's doing her. This type of woman has feelings that are not only guarded but trapped within her. She's been mistreated, left out, left behind, and doubted. She has a high sex drive and has been fatherless or motherless for many years, her emotions are easily controlled, and sometimes, she seems *emotionless*—yet she yearns for respect.

She's a quick-mouthed woman, which makes a man either want to physically abuse her, leave her, or verbally abuse her. Most of these women are left in the relationship, but most times, the men come back, even the married ones. She's comfortable to be with and be around, simply because of two things: she won't tell on you and will never cause a scene. She's the woman that does to men what men do to women, and men can't stand or handle that. It's a weird sense of deep attraction and respect because she's just as detached as the broken men, which causes us not to have *any* control over her, what she says, and how she feels. You'll always hear the man say "I can respect that" knowing very well that he can't yet his feelings are growing deeper and deeper!

These women can easily manipulate and deceive men, just like we do to women. In a lot of cases, while involved with women like this, we're okay being the second, third, or even fourth man in her life. One man may offer her sex, another may offer her money, one may bring the kids food and diapers while another other will provide weed, alcohol, and drives her back and forth from the airport to see her "out of town dude" who we won't even know. She has "female" friends in many states—99% of them are "males"!

Respect is at the back of her mind, but she doesn't expect to offer that to anyone. Her idea of love can be physical abuse, verbal abuse, and a lack of time and attention—things that are deeply rooted in the absence of her parents. She, on many occasions, becomes okay with arguing and make-up sex. This woman is very attractive because she will not hold any man accountable, likes simple things, cooks well, and offers sex at any given time of the day. She'll perform oral sex in the car, at a red light, at your job, the movie theater, and most places that a girlfriend or wife won't. For about three to six months, —sometimes even longer depending on how dysfunctional and unhappy the man is with his partner—this woman will receive financial support as well. She becomes part of the budget! This woman does have a hard time using men like men use women and she'll eventually find the man of her dreams because from her experiences, she's not only had plenty of men but was also building her man off of those she knows or have been with. Once she commits, she's very solid and trustworthy—she's seen it all!

The Easy-Pleasing Man

Drives women crazy – never on purpose, but they will never say anything in protest. Has a lot of ways that are just like the "Easy-Pleasing Woman." He's been hurt in relationships and seems very nonchalant. Usually has gone through a nasty divorce and doesn't want much, and is very hesitant to take or receive from women. Very guarded but likes a variety of things, including women. Easy to get along with, speaks well, and is a deep thinker and listener. Has lost a lot in life and is very cautious. He can be very cool, calm, and reserved, yet very slick about many things. Loves women, but is slow to commit. He has a lot of his own stuff, may share, but can also be very stingy!

This type of man will make women wonder about themselves; although not deliberate, it takes him a while to open up. Some women may feel like he doesn't like them or isn't interested. That's not the case, it's just that his past has hurt him, and he will have a hard time trusting women. He has done some deep soul-searching over the years and his growth can be attractive. This man has plenty of female friends, some platonic and some sexual, but he has become extremely honest with all of them, a trait that he never had before. It's been a long time for him, but he now trusts himself. Honesty is at the forefront of his mind now, and sometimes, it can be brutal.

His sex drive has slowed down some, not due to age or health, but because he now requires passion, compassion, and has more of a desire to make love than casual sex. As he gets older, this man becomes more monogamous than anything. He may look at other women, not in a lustful way, but in a way that assesses what she wears or how she looks, which may interest him in asking "*what do you think about her hair or outfit?*" Or he may just buy that outfit or jewelry for you. He's gawking at women; it's a respectful thing because he pays attention to things you like or may like. Women can see how genuine he is and that he possesses the traits they have been wanting and seeking for years. This man has great conversations, is open about his past, and wants a great, healthy future. Due to his past mistakes, he will sometimes consider an old relationship to go back to.

The Head Down

There are plenty of men and women who put their head down when their partners raise their voices, or when the accusations of cheating keep coming up. For the woman, she's been beaten down over and over and wonders why she can't be put on a pedestal and respected—he can't! This woman has accepted being put down, berated, and disrespected, so much so that the kids disrespect her too. You have determined what the kids see and hear, and it has been passed down to them.

On most occasions, when a woman becomes quiet and bows her head, her partner or husband is the issue, but she just can't put her finger on it. At this point, it's time for you to realize that it's something that was passed to him, probably sixty to seventy years ago, and has nothing to do with you, yet you have been the target of *his* generational curse. When you ask questions or suggest help, you become the "bad wife/girlfriend." It will not end while you are with him, unless you find yourself, courage, and self-esteem—and you can.

Sometimes, we see these people coming and sometimes, we can't see them going. This is where women end up in a casket. Surround yourself with people that have come out of these situations, and those that have regained their own identity, with reference to how they were raised, their parents' fifty-year marriage, and your genetics, less a generational curse. You just might have married into one. Some men are just *waiting* to enjoy the real you; they see you, give hints, subtle compliments, and not the one that was created by someone that only knows how to beat you down mentally. Sometimes you have to take a small chance, just a little at a time. Doing so, you'll gain more confidence in knowing that you still have it, you just gave it up temporarily to give yourself, the kids, and him, a chance at a wonderful life. But some men don't want that, they'd rather have a slave!

The only time your head is up is when you're in bed, staring at the ceiling, either afraid to go to sleep or wondering why you have become this shell of a woman. You know it's not right, yet you hold onto the wrong. To his friends, you've become a cunt or a bitch, sometimes you hear the words, feel them, but over the years, you've accepted it, all from an abuser that causes you to start abusing yourself!

Pull your head up so you can see the people who will love you uncondition- ally, guide you, and rehabilitate you. Let them pull you out of the quick- sand before it turns into cement, where you'll be suspended and stuck. More importantly, allow those people who will help you become that beautiful person and future grandmother and keep you out of the morgue!

The man has also married or is engaged to a woman who feels like her mother's way is the best way to treat her man. She infuses her beliefs into the relationship without even considering how her man was raised and what he thinks or believes. The woman also carries forward issues from her last relationship, comparing her current man to her last man. He can't say much, but he will, and it will fall on deaf ears. This woman will always compare you to her father, both good and bad; yet you're not her father, nor do you share his genetics.

You'll constantly feel like a caged lion – lost, and left out – and her family will expect you to follow suit with their lifestyle. You can't do anything right in her and their eyes. Once you have children, she'll want to control them too. It almost makes you want to start a whole new family over again. Her friends and the aunt that her family don't like will see the genuine man in you and warn you to leave.

Again, surround yourself with men that have been in this type of relationship as well, get your confidence, friends and family back, and don't be afraid to seek people that really care about you and will seek better partners for you.

She'll be happy one week, and angry the next, then swears she's ok, but won't tell you the truth. Some of these women have been molested by men in the family and have never gotten help. Not getting help after being molested or raped will cause your sex life with her to be painful, boring, fear-induced, lacking knowledge of sex, and damn near non-existent.

The two of you should get help so that she can trust you and have a healthy relationship, knowing that you know her deep fears and secrets, yet you accept and respect her and are ready to grow together. It's not an end-all. She needs to know that you love her—unconditionally. She'll want to cry on your shoulder. She does love you, but her family and their truth seem to be the right way. It just might be, but that's only half of the truth! Her family is her security blanket, but you must be her security cameras that protect her exterior, in addition to her warm family blanket! They should not be allowed to choose her man for her, so you'll have to play a major part in getting her to believe in you. Cry with her, protect her, hold her, and look into her eyes to feel her soul, spirit, and the voids that have long been empty—refill them with trust and healing.

Pale and Dark - Be proud of your skin color. Throughout the years, I've heard people say some truly disgusting things about other people with pale or dark skin. Thank God that I wasn't raised that way. I'll begin with the skin counter against prejudices. Love your *Pale* and *Dark* skin, as your skin is the largest, living organ you have. Let the prejudiced people admire all of you, flaunt it, be proud of it, and wear it well. Stay away from tans, as this will harm your beauty. Be you, and show others that you enjoy being in the skin that God gave you, and not them. Truthfully, there are people that are deeply attracted to your Pale, Dark, loving, original beauty. It's the contrast that becomes alluring to them. You stand out because you are unique. For the pale skin, your color goes with ANY color; that's just one of the many strengths you have. If you choose to do anything, something you feel that may enhance your beauty, wear a nice, soft, or even colorful, hair color. Lipstick that matches works well too. You'll be surprised what colors will do for your ravishing, gorgeous, heavenly, stunning, irresistible, beguiling, winsome, and charming gift!

For the dark beauty, the same goes for you! Embrace your magical, appealing, mind-shocking, attractive, pleasing, and utterly tasteful wonder! Burnt orange sits well in your hair and lips, so does burgundy, or auburn. Platinum and silver are exotic colors as well that can be very electrifying! Consider yourself a cherished anomaly, one that is extraordinarily extravagant! You radiate and exude power, you bring light, joy, and energy to people. People look and stare because they are drawn to you – allow them to admire! You have a magnetic force field surrounding you that most cannot resist. The Pale and Dark are extremely rare and distinct—embrace your flair and continue to show up!

Overweight – *Y*ou're not overweight, you need to be *over them*. You are full and voluptuous. Trust me, there's no need to be ashamed and looking for ways to lose weight to make someone else happy, or to even keep someone in your life. I know a lot of men and women that enjoy a more "full figured" partner. The weight that most people are intimidated by, is your *mental weight*, intellect! Full figured people, the ones that I have met, have been extremely confident. It's like those that lose their eyesight, or their hearing, they encompass other traits that are strong and attractive and become even more useful and beneficial to their life, so use your weight! We all have areas or things we can improve in our lives, so keep that in mind. You are who you are, but there are many exceptional qualities that you have inherited. You must find out what they are and then get rid of the excess negativity that society has imposed on you. Know and appreciate every curve of your body because men do. By societal standards, even at 215 pounds, I am considered obese, yet I refuse to allow any external forces or stressors to steer myself clear of what I know to be useful and special talents. You can rule in any setting, your personality is huge, big, colorful, vivacious, and to some, overwhelming – much better than being… underwhelming. You have been given many talents, so use them. Transform your body weight into the weight you have in success, love, and your positive effect in inspiring others!

Married into Success - These women and men are very reserved because of all of the VIP treatment they receive and the general expectation to be someone they're not! You have nice things, just like the "Rich Homemaker" but you can't really enjoy it. You did enjoy it at one time, and that was years ago, before your partner reminded you of how they built their empire before you.

"This is mine and if we ever go to court, or get divorced…I'll do everything in my power to ruin you. My friends know I had this before you!"

The woman or man *married into success* has gone years suffering and they have now realized that money "will not" *buy you happiness*, but it will *loan you sadness!* They only want the small things in life; a kiss, to be held, respected, and recognized. After a few or many years, all they want is their simple life back! The acting has now become…aching!

S.I – Super Independent men and women, although they have their stuff together, still miss out. In their previous relationships, they were so unimportant, insignificant, that they pushed so hard to get their identity back. They've become hermits of sorts in their own world and mind. You have to remember that we all want and need reassuring confidence so do not bypass the ones that want to genuinely be with you. Over time, you've proven that you can do it all by yourself, but remember, you've been a giver, sideshow, trophy, arm girl, etc. You've played the role well, mostly by being real and honest, so you do possess the traits to be a life-partner. Don't allow your past to ruin your favorite pastime – and that is being present 100% with your legitimate 100 percent-er!

The Lead-on - The first words out of their mouths without thinking are; *Yea, Hell Yea, I'm down, I swear, seriously, trust me when I tell you, for real, I kid you not.* These words are called "replacers" or 'fillers". This is an act of stalling you, to make you think before you catch them in a lie. They're persona is extremely obvious on most occasions because their inner weakness shows through an embarrassing smile or their next words, "What's wrong, or "You good?" Lead on people are always chasing their tail but want to believe that they're not. They are also very nosey and basically gather information to make themselves look good or to appear real. Lead-ons know when people are onto them but self manipulate so that they think no one really knows, everyone does, except them.

The Abused - Men and women that are or have been abused, for whatever reason, can be cold, quiet, calculating, vindictive and many more things. On the contrary, they want to be open, honest, and understood. On many occasions, they carry hurt and pain through life. Abused people have a low tolerance for disrespect, dishonesty, liars, cheaters and many more people that remind them of those that hurt them. Their triggers are in the front of their mind and they remain guarded. They require extensive knowledge about you but are reserved to giving up much information about themselves. They open up slowly. Some have mental reservations about sex, speaking openly, giving advice, and taking chances. Abused people are very careful listeners, and they process words and actions in a measured way. Most are overprotective and very slow to get close to people.

"AS A BROKEN MAN, I WANTED A VARIETY OF WOMEN—BUT QUICKLY FOUND OUT THAT, WOMEN WANT A MAN WITH VARIETIES."

~ LEON R. WALKER JR~

Chapter Thirty

Men Cheat Down; Women Cheat Up

Some women step out. A lot of times, it's after the man has done so. They'll even replicate his process to make it hurt even more! The "cheating up" plan—because it is a plan—is treacherous. Women hold interviews and the "mister" doesn't even know. Men don't interview, our plan is to get right to sex. The mistress is a provider of small things and she usually has low self-esteem, an EBT card, and a few children. In most cases, she's a safe bet but has other men too. You're not supposed to fall in love with the "other", but we do because she makes life easier and stress-free. Only because she's the path of "least resistance," doesn't have any marriage morals, and will *not* hold us accountable.

Her home doesn't require maintenance and in any case, she could care less about housekeeping. Sex is unlimited, food is scarce and her main concern is hair weave, lace fronts, some weed, Hennessy, and a ride to drop the kids off.

The "loyal wife" holds this title proudly but we take her for granted. Once we get caught, we'll lose a lot of her. She'll stay, on most occasions, but will only be sixty percent in the marriage, if at all. She'll eventually file for divorce. Meanwhile, the man that she's eyeing is taller, bigger, has a great job, a nice car, and people speak well of him. You'll see him indirectly but will not have a clue about who he really is. She'll have you around him and you won't even know. If you are all in the same place, she will not be publicly intimate with you in public; she'll spend the time with you but will have him on her mind. Most times, you will not catch her looking at him for a couple of reasons: she knows that you're watching her because of your infidelity and because she wants to keep him around for as long as she can. Don't think for one minute that when you have sex, she's into it because of you. She's not, he's motivating her mind from a distance!

If she's sure that he can keep a secret, her new infatuation might be the local police officer, cable guy, mechanic, your child's teacher or principal—someone that either comes to the house or that you'll have to see or meet and not know. You'll surely go to report card pickup with her and sit right across from him, smiling!

Men, those that are "Players" cheat down and take the path of *least resistance,* to avoid the path of *most resistance.* Women cheat, up and take the path of *most resistance,* she does this to test him and make sure he's solid and ok with being her secret. When we cheat down, the "Mistress" will want to come up and be treated like "The Wife." As for the woman that cheats up, her "Mister" will not allow himself to, nor will she let or bring him down, he'll receive what you're not getting and she'll keep him UP, while holding you...DOWN! You'll become a void filler, the old voids that you've become comfortable with filling. Since she has a "Mister" your void filling will not mean anything to her! She'll make you think you're doing something, when in all actuality, you're now just a "role" player. Once she stops complaining, it doesn't mean that you're good, it means that he's better! She's vulnerable.

I never want to see anyone go through this. Men or women, the pain is too much. This was a chin check for me, as I could not take it. An extreme, heart-wrenching, gut punch for me. Back then, I wasn't in the right frame of mind, and although it hurt to see him, it was very easy to call him ugly. I had to see him to ease my pain. His lack of looks, didn't work because that wasn't the root cause or the cause of my pain, losing her was, he still had her, and I didn't. He wasn't ugly, though. I was the one that was ugly, speaking from my inner being. To her, he was beautiful, and looking back on it, I can see it now, he was. It wasn't about looks, which I was all about that and being that way, for years I would miss the mark on understanding women, from within, both her and I. You will too if you don't look deeper into your lady and what she possesses, but more importantly, what she needs and when she needs it, seeking beyond her physical appearance. Men need this too. Your partner is well aware of their looks but the internal growth needs to be cultivated, even if it's just holding hands, something I never did, but the ugly dude did. When a person is vulnerable, it stems from their lack of, not attaining, or being depleted of their emotional needs, and not looks!

Recovery

As far as transitioning from the hurt and pain, there are four phases that you are not only required to be familiar with, but you must make yourself available for all of them, irregardless of your mindset during this transition.

Forming. Your new mindset to deal with all levels of impending uncertainty, be honest with yourself and don't be afraid to call yourself out.

Storming. Your storm will become part of your daily existence. You must be resilient. You control the length of time your storm remains as long you are brutally honest. While in your storm, people will see the hurt in your face and body language, it's ok, it belongs to you but will subside. I'm not saying to not seek counsel, but it's imperative to seek out people that have gone through this, close and understanding friends. Stay away from alcohol, find a hobby, don't be afraid to cry, because you will cry. During these days, weeks, or even months, you are living with four things;

Accepting the path of most resistance.

Always take it head on. It's going to hurt, but the hurt will lessen as long as you remain in truth and take responsibility.

Standing in the "Shadows of Love."

While standing, you are not ready to love anyone, yet beginning to love your soon to be "true self" and making profound changes! This is not the time to fall, yet it is the time to stand tall and proud in the face of adversity!

The feeling of Temptation

Stop the negative thoughts of calling excessively to your partner. Remember, they have a four phase season, too. Do not seek out songs of love and sorrow, this will make you reminisce.

Acts of neglect

Refuse the desire to binge eat just to make yourself feel better and fill your stomach to sleep it off. This causes you to avoid reality, this being counter-productive. Do your best to push past laziness and workout. Join running or walking groups. Continue to pay into yourself by keeping your hair done, beard trimmed, haircut, nails done, and consistent upkeep of hygiene. *Do not* neglect the kids, if you have any. Once you are with your kids, make it all about them and do not ask them about their mother or father and who they're seeing. kids are deeply affected when parents aren't getting along or going through a divorce or separation.

Mourning. Dealing with the loss, less the blame and finger-pointing.

Norming. The time to reflect *and* accept that you can't be the same person you were in the hurting or lack of discipline stages. Norming will later bring you to seek the following.

Relationship Internship = For many years, we have associated "Internship" with college and work. In relationships, the *internship* stage becomes a true trial and journey that we must implement to misdirect the belief of the old and consistently used adage "work internship" to know where we must implement it. This is for proper alignment, placement, and selection. I will now speak about this, too.

A, or the position of a student or trainee who is in the 'workings" status of an organization, the organization being "organizing the relationship, *not your future job,* in an effort to gain experience or satisfy requirements for qualification! This is a must for both personell and should not be avoided! By being an intern, we are in that "company" or in the "company" of that person. We are now better prepared to become accustomed to that person in many facets of their wants, needs, desires, and their personality.

JUST SMILE

Just smile for a while, I love your smile.

It took me a while to let you know—your smile is why I smile.

Like the cool smell of your body scent,

heaven-sent, message went

across my face when I saw you smile—and for a while.

You bring me joy, strength, peace, happiness,

your smile removes me from my dizziness, craziness, loneliness.

Bring that smile, and give me that kiss, a wish

to see that smile, so I can cherish

this, and then hold me, push me back, look at me,

so I can see, your beautiful face,

but more importantly your smile, your taste,

that smile puts me in my place, total grace!

"MAKE ME YOUR HUSBAND. MORE
OFTEN THAN NOT, WE HEAR THE WORDS,
'WHEN ARE YOU GOING TO MAKE HER
YOUR WIFE?' HARDLY EVER DO WE
HEAR 'MAKE ME YOUR HUSBAND.' I
WOULD LIKE TO SEE MANY CHANGES
IN THE WORLD, BUT ONE THAT I HAVE
IN MIND IS THE DAY WHEN MEN YEARN
LIKE WOMEN AND ASK, 'WHEN ARE
YOU GOING TO MAKE ME YOUR HUS-
BAND?' SOME OF US JUST WANT TO BE
FATHERS ONLY!"

~ LEON R. WALKER JR~

Chapter Thirty One

Growing and Climbing in Love

Growing and Climbing in love takes time. As humans, we've spoken at length and taught the world about "Falling in Love," and I've perceived that the concept itself has been rather misleading. The concept of "falling," together with the word "failing," connotes a downward trend, regardless of how you look at it. When you fall or fail, your heart sinks, your head falls, your eyes may even close, and your doubts emerge!

I now speak on *Climbing* and *Growing* in Love! *Upward mobility, agility, and ability*!

"YOU GROW TO LOVE PEOPLE, AND YOU LOVE TO GROW PEOPLE."

~ LEON R. WALKER JR~

The foremost deed you must be willing to do, to climb and grow in love with your partner, is to spend honest time in their presence and natural environment, *observing*. While existing and basking in their pure essence, take a moment to acknowledge as many features as you can. Express some, but maintain a stronghold on others. Women are time released, and as men, we primarily look to release without any sense of timing! We must begin to live and acknowledge in a timely fashion in an effort to understand and introduce ourselves to many things. First, by having an apprehensive approach to letting go or giving in too early to any temptation, and secondly, by knowing and understanding the "time releasing" of a woman, a mechanism which creates a world of comfort for the two of you.

Don't give too much, too soon. You don't want to appear desperate. You'll never fall in love with a man or woman because of just one thing; it's virtually impossible. If you do, or think that you are in love, I assure you that it's not love but lust. When you exist in lust, you become more interested in something *you* like and not in anything they exhibit. Furthermore, you'll find yourself dependent, absorbed, and devoted to being insubstantial in recognizing real beauty. In addition, while lusting, there will be a form of neglect of either their favorite quality or one that they don't know about or don't like if they do know about it. As a friend and companion, it's your job to make them aware of many most doted on and cherished possessions, and even more so, the least likely qualities or traits that they hide or aren't aware of.

More often than not, we home in on the obvious body parts; large breasts, muscles, nice lips, sculptured buttocks, a pretty face, handsome men, athletic builds or easily accessible traits, the ones we either choose to exude or allow to take precedence. These body parts and traits are what most of us keep readily available because they're tied to our self-esteem and confidence, and with societal norms dictating the mindsets of many, we tend to be easily influenced by counterfeit people that retain superficial and shallow desires that render us incapable of realizing that we withhold many more attractive characteristics and attributes. By thinking, caring, and performing in a manner different from those less-likely people who don't understand or are simply complimenting, we gain trust, cohesiveness, open communication and inseparable chemistry which removes reticent behavior, ensuring an awareness that reveals a much deeper attraction. Over the years of my therapy and soul searching, I have come to know and enjoy the following traits of women outside of my once basic and inept mindset:

- A confident walk
- A crooked smile
- Different shaped eyes and ears
- A beautiful personality
- Honesty
- Shyness possessing ability
- Very understanding with a passionate response
- A woman unfazed by others
- A woman that knows her place as a woman, but can exchange roles to support her man
- A woman that enjoys being a mother but knows when to be a partner
- A woman that can and will indirectly inform you about people that are not good for you
- Independent but lets you know of her desires
- Classy
- Can be heard while silent
- A woman that speaks with her eyes

"GROWING IN LOVE" IS A PLAN, A GOAL, JUST LIKE ANYTHING ELSE IN THIS WORLD THAT YOU WANT TO BE SUC-CESSFUL AT, BUT YOU MUST FIRST BE REAL ABOUT IT AND READY. YOU HAVE TO STUDY, PREPARE, TAKE NOTES, HAVE A VISION, AND ENJOY THE COURSE. WHILE GROWING IN ANY ASPECT TAKES TIME, PATIENCE, ENCOURAGEMENT, CULTIVATION, CARE, AND PASSION, YOU MUST HOWEVER MAKE SURE YOU'RE *CLIMBING AND GROWING9AND* NOT *FALLING* IN LOVE!

~ LEON R. WALKER JR~

Chapter Thirty Two

The Ships

FRIEND-SHIP – This must be established first before anything else. Always remember, looks aren't everything; a beautiful personality beats a pretty face, every time. Some people look good in relationships, even in a marriage, but do they feel good?

Build a true and genuine friendship! Developing this, you learn about one another, inside and out. You'll tell the truth without embarrassment, secrets, or regrets. There will be an abundance of understanding, relating, and discussions. This is where listening to each other is learned; not over-talking but sharing ideas. Whether the relationship will take off or not is determined by whether the listening stage does or does not develop anytime during the friendship stage. This will spur each other's growth by knowing both of your desires, wants, needs, dislikes, and triggers. Converse about friends, family, associates, and what turns you off and on. The motivation not to hurt a person starts with a great friendship. You must be loyal and committed to them in everything. This also means telling them the truth, even when it hurts. Although it may hurt, your delivery is just as important as your message!

COURT-SHIP - Dating is compulsory, and this does not mean just going to restaurants. It's okay to share your favorite places to go and the foods and drinks that you like, but a date must include odd places. You have to understand that your future partner lives by a different culture and women not only enjoy learning, but they also do not want to be or remain mentally stagnant or stuck.

Being spontaneous is great too. Get into what the other person enjoys, even if it's your first time. Call often but not too much. Have respect for their personal time and do not be offended if they're not totally available when you want their time. It's great if they explain why but what's more important is that you do not become upset. Courting is a very intricate and intimate time. You must always fall back on the memories of your friendship period. It's crucial to remember that courting is a derivative of friendship and that they do not mean to hurt your feelings when they are not available. If you listen and care deeply, with intent, in the friendship stages, you will avoid many issues later on. Sometimes, courting is the buildup to a relationship later on. That person may just as well, be from your past but at the time of trying to date, just wasn't the time. You'll be drawn back to that person, over and over again.

COMPANION-SHIP - Company is very soothing, especially with someone who knows and understands you. Being in the company of a person is supposed to be comforting, with an exchange of thoughts, ideas, plans, and goals. It's about combined success, just like a successful company. The morale has to be high, and it must also have morals, rules, regulations, finances, budgets, and a low turnover ratio. It is a meeting of minds. It doesn't have to be called a meeting; it could be a lunch date to speak about the future, growth, longevity, and possibly branching out—expanding the family!

LEADER-SHIP - It's imperative that couples know about and learn their Emotional Intelligence—what it is and what it means.

EMIQ = Passion, Compassion, Courage, Empathy.

Be passionate about your partner and what they like, love, and enjoy. If you're not passionate about what they are passionate about, you must be compassionate about their passion! Have the courage to let them know you may not like it, but be sensitive enough to try to like it. If you still don't like it, have the courage to respect their life choices. We're not talking about anything toxic here; they are all positive things. However, if there are some toxins, they must be discussed and dealt with. This brings me to discuss the last component of EMIQ.

Being empathetic allows you to listen, take in, respond, relate, be aware of, but most importantly, understand without becoming emotionally involved. When you become emotionally involved, you lose your ability to convey your feelings from your heart and mind. Instead, you may begin to feel sorry for your partner. They don't need your pity; they need understanding with a way ahead or a solution, with examples of how you overcame what they couldn't, thus freeing their minds of any fear or doubt.

"I understand how you feel. I've felt the same way." By saying this, you can build a person's willpower with analogies and even your truth, for transparency.

Also, another ingredient is being willing to discuss, being aware of and injecting an exchange of power—it's crucial in a relationship. There is a difference between power and horsepower.

Power is granted to you by a job title, team, or military. Going into a relationship, power isn't just given up or away. In some cases, people go in thinking they have all of the power. Usually, this person has some insecurities that are deeply rooted. They've been used or abused. You should never just relinquish any power. I do not recommend calling it power, I prefer the term knowledge. No matter what you call it, it can be abused, but should not be! Some people earn power, some chase it, while some receive it by virtue of their title. In a relationship, power must be understood, distributed equally and fairly, and known.

We all have different levels of power and weaknesses. This is where the exchange or shift has to play an integral part in order to maintain cohesiveness, unity, and continuity. Power can be lost but not knowledge, unless there's some form of injury, trauma, or mental health concerns. Either way, one has to take over and maintain what has been built and exchanged. This is why power is exchanged not for the sole purpose of giving, but for knowing what the other person knows or forgets. We are both the same when it comes to our knowledge base; at one point, you may know more than I do, but we're in this to bring each other up to par.

Power - Has a sense of weakness to it when taken or accepted for the wrong reasons. Some people become anxious to receive it in an effort to belittle, demean, hurt, harm, or control others. Using it like this will make you lose it, along with your companion.

Horsepower - Much better and stronger. Horsepower is gained when your heart, mind, body, and spirit are aligned for the right reasons. Greed, lust, and envy are all nonexistent. Horsepower is granted when a person is intimate with a noble cause. Virtues that come with horsepower include peace, team-building, the love of people, caring deeply, and a concern for life, family, and a work-life balance. When you live as a good-natured person, this will be granted to you. There will be no need to expect it, it's coming. All you have to do is to be aware of this blessing because not everyone will receive it. It's a spiritual title that comes with enlightenment, down-pouring, and filling. Living right, your soul will be open for special gifts and closed off from hatred, doubt, lethargy, haste, and all evil intent. Relationships that have horsepower become much happier and healthier, with a clearer vision, focus, and future. Everything will be in place and the synergy will resonate with you both, on every level! There will not be any individual elements.

Chapter Thirty Three

Seasons and Reasons

Seasons and Reasons coexist, not just with the partnerships you have in life, but also throughout your life experience. I truly believe that there is never a period in life when these concepts do not exist and play out in our lives, nor do I believe that there is a way to avoid them. In fact, you should never attempt to. Many people are unaware of how they support and balance each other out as "sustainers with sustenance" when their understanding and interrelation are simultaneous. This interrelation and mindset is pure and beautiful. A lot of people have given up, but you shouldn't, because there are great men and women that possess great qualities that can compliment you. Speaking for myself, with reference to rebuilding, I was a man that was by far the most toxic, unhappy, dysfunctional, irrational, unfair, lost, and sick—and if I could change and grow into wanting better, doing better, but more importantly, seeing better, then any man or woman can do it too. These are not only key components of the concepts of Seasons and Reasons, but the relationships that function in this manner, exist as very high-performing and high-functioning with minimal dysfunction or distraction.

Although this timeframe may seem like a period characterized by just *undertakings and actions*, it's actually who we are and how we act or react during this term that matters. Seasons and Reasons carry emotions, thoughts, insights, hindsight, awareness, and energy. It can be positive, but could also harbor an acute sense of the negative when there's a malfunction. Most people avoid or barely pay any attention to this, nor do they discuss the elements enough. To "ask" a person what season of their life they're in, shows a level of care and concern and can also give a person that understands seasons and reasons a feeling of synchronization.

I've noticed and experienced, in a lot of situations, that most people may not even know what season they're in, causing their partner to observe with uncertainty, bewilderment, or perplexity. There's nothing more disheartening than having a partner that is off kilter, bygone, or emotionally detached because of their inability to be acquainted.

There are many variables to *seasons* and *reasons*, but, by far the most important, is a visceral acknowledgment of one's *Love Language.*

Love the Season and Know the Reason for the Language

You should enjoy and continue to love and speak to one another during bad times, just as much and as respectfully as during the good times—by understanding who your partner is at that time. Not only knowing who they are, but affording yourself the opportunity to be an advocate, owning the mastery of cognizant, adsorption, and assimilation qualities, and having the perception to identify less- loving energies. The less-loving energies aren't displayed on purpose, but they are built on many external forces. You must know how to capitalize on the negative so that you may reduce its power of nullifying any reduction your connectivity and magnetic forces of chemistry are constructing. This builds longevity and staying power!

The most important, and extremely invaluable knowledge here, is that of one's attributes and criteria, along with when and where one's seasons show up. Although some people believe, some still don't, and this is a crucial mistake that we all make when starting a relationship of any sort. In an effort to acquire the utmost level of understanding, reasoning, love, reciprocity, connection, affection, intimacy, and chemistry from your friend, partner, family, kids, employees, employer, school officials, teachers, and any other educators, you must first understand yours and their seasons and the compatibility between them, while employing discernment and empathy.

Regardless of what your labor or exertion is during your season, it is paramount that you become intricately involved with yourself and your season, coupled with an ability to not only convey such, but also to refine the manner by which you deliver it. Without an aptitude or a way to bespeak, you will surely have a season, as aforementioned, but without a clear and identified reason. Seasons ebb and flow, yet during that time, we must make adjustments to our relationships with people, our feelings, thoughts, vision, focus, proposals, intentions, goals, and objectives, but first, we must be real and sincere in our quest.

The Season – A person's season encompasses many things:

- Who they are
- How they were raised
- How they act during their season
- How they feel
- What they feel
- What their journey is about
- Clarity
- Spiritual connection
- Their beliefs
- Sexual desires
- Various wants of intimacy
- A complete understanding of their universal connection
- A heart rid of discontent and weight

The understanding segment takes place during the first encounter, whether in a meeting, a job interview, casual encounters, or when engaging in a conversation.

The "season" aspect that I am about to discuss, has many levels, feelings, emotions, visions, and thought processes. Like I mentioned earlier, while this may seem mundane to some or many, it's not only crucial, but essential to life itself. The universe, seasons, nature, and spiritual/soul alignment plays an integral part in both balance and in contending with/understanding an impending or current "imbalance" of either yourself or people that you *may* or *will* come in contact with, encounter, marry, date, work with, lead, or follow.

You may find that it may be quite cumbersome, confusing, or even tough to do—yes, there will be challenges, but it's not confusing, tough, or cumbersome. Once you read, understand, and adhere to all I have said and will continue to write here, and make this "Season-Reason" lesson a part of your life, then there will be many things that will happen for you. For those women and men that are time-sensitive, time-released, or intricately time-related, speaking of punctuality on many levels, this will resonate with you, because when you literally "show up" ready in someone's life, you do so during and for a Season and Reason. This will be extremely profound, liberating, and can create chemistry on a level so engaging and enlightening that you will come to know and understand true love, unity, and connections. With that being said, my lessons will equip those women and men with the ability to reduce the amount of time wasted in developing someone – be it a man or woman – over long periods of time, or grooming them for your standards or even their potential, and preparing the two of you for a more healthy, fulfilling life journey, whether it's a friendship or relationship!

We have all probably experienced people who feel so "magnetic." Well, there's a reason why. So, while showing up, don't expect anything but equality and fairness, for starters, and if the person can't grant you those, coupled with reciprocity, then let them know and move on, but do not close that door, as you, *the one that showed up,* are also a teacher and developer of those that haven't quite gotten to your level. "Magnetic or Glue people" are those that are already on their journey. Just remember, we can all attain that level, it just might not be our *season* at that moment. Do not desist from holding their inability to connect with you at that moment against them or you will slowly lose your gift. The gift you have or the work that you put into achieving that level is used to help and incorporate those with the potential to be by your side or in your life, in any way. If no one else poured into you or prepared you, God has, and it doesn't get any more pristine, refined, authentic, and genuine than that.

When you unfold, your glow and energy will precede you. You must be aware of this, but more importantly, know that it can and will intimidate those that are not ready for your presence or powerful existence. You'll know this as well. Continue to pay into these people without reservation, extending small gestures, because you can't help or avoid giving back since you are now the teacher and messenger. There's a reason for still paying into those that you feel are either less likely to take heed or do not deserve your time or effort, which is understandable. So, the "reason" (there's the word again) behind you paying into them is because it will lessen your worries about them "showing up" in your life each time with negative energy. As you are now a magnanimous person, they tend to re-think each and every moment of time they're around you. They either become better or bitter, depending on how they receive you. Your aura will be their deter-minant and vehicle for whether to remain or leave. By paying into them, you pay into yourself, and it won't be a waste of your time whilst making room for those that are meant to be with or around you, those who choose to remain in your vehicle. People that can't or aren't ready, won't! Your gift or growth will pull from them what you are supposed to see, and feel. How so? Here's a list of Reasons:

- That individual or those people will seem nervous around you.
- Tap-dancing around you or your questions and decisions.

- Their body language will be erratic and shifty.

- They will leave your company or avoid you.

- They will lie for no reason, trying to impress you.

- Their time is never in tune with yours.

- They will always have horrible excuses, many of them.

- You won't feel any sort of connection.

- You will never get butterflies around this person, yet you will feel very uneasy.

- Their discussions will not interest you.

- Instant turn-offs will appear to you. This can be a bit unfair, but pay attention to it.

- There will be more turn-offs than turn-ons.

- If you do perhaps give them a chance, the letdowns will be insurmountable.

- This relationship will be a total waste of your time and most signs will rear their ugly heads within minutes of meeting this person.

- They have a draining appearance and personality.

- These people will have more questions than answers.

- They're needy, and once you fill one of their voids, they'll leave.

- They will not compliment you, and if they do, it'll lack substance and passion.

These are just some of the negative signs that you'll get. Some of the positive signs for people that are on the same journey or those that are reaching your level are:

- They'll seem quite comfortable in your presence.

- The eye contact will be constant.

- They'll listen intently to you.

- Their questions will be well thought-out.

- They give you uncommon compliments.

- They pay attention to you.

- They will share ideas with you.

- They're prompt.

- They keep their word.

- Their plans will include you.

- They will consult you.

- Your advice will help them grow.

- You'll take their advice.

- You can see a future with them.

- Your ideas coincide.

- There will hardly ever be any disagreements; if there are, you'll both politely come to a resolution – one that benefits both parties.

- Neither of you will feel like you have to "one-up" the other.

I feel that these are the most common "Reasons," for identifying most, if not all relationships, and what they encompass.

In concluding this section, knowing your season and being aware of the reason comes from traits that we all have, so never accept an excuse from a person that feels like they "just can't" with you. If they do feel that way, then they're right, and don't waste your time with them. Here are some traits you can look out for and that can be violated during your Season and Reasoning:

- Listening.

- Studying people.

- Asking thought-provoking questions.

- Observing habits.

- Paying attention to timing, as timing is usually associated with alignment.

- Awareness of Menstrual cycle season. This is a short, possibly weekly season. As for the man's cycle, because we do have one, it's a time of needing reassuring confidence when avoiding our feminine side, as we so often do. A woman's reminder is her intuition, one we pay attention to when all else fails. It's our lifeline. It happens.

- Showing affection.

- Learning psychological reciprocity.

As I have mentioned in earlier parts of the book, Love Languages are an integral part of every season. Some say there are five while some say seven. The thing though is that it doesn't matter how many there are; once you know yours and your partner's, you have to act accordingly.

- *Words of affirmation* – Pay attention to your partner's strengths but also to the things they need to work on. Be careful how you extend any recommendations as to what they need to work on. Those "needs to work on" can be spoken about as a strength but which just requires a little more effort. Different compliments are better than the usual compliments. When you take the time to see different things in her or him, you build their confidence and show them that you see what others or themselves haven't seen. This is by far the best form of complimenting your partner. Stay away from the norm!

- *Quality time* – Women place this language above most others, although it's interrelated with other love languages. With reference to how you do what you do, it's not just quality time but timing—as in, *when* you spend that time. There should never be a time limit on quality time. The key word is "quality", but just as important is the location where that time is spent. Be resourceful, spontaneous, thoughtful, original, creative, and put energy into your quality time plans.

- *Acts of service* – Return a favor, but make it better and give more than what you received. Do not take too much time returning the favor, because time is sensitive here. Add a nice note or thank you card with the favor. Give back to her or him, and include their pet or a loved one. This is how you give more. Be cognizant of what they are missing, and pay attention to what's being depleted from their life.

- *Physical touch* – Take the time to learn their body, wants, needs, and desires. Never be basic, greedy or selfish. Do not compete, and listen to what they like. They are not your last partner. It's not always about actual sex—sex is with the eyes, words, appreciation; these are related to being "sexy". It comes in many other forms as well, respect, support, uplifting, protection, caring, knowing, and learning from your partner. Putting him or her first. The 'touch' part is focusing on their heart, soul, spirit, and mind. These are all "Non-sexual" but just as powerful as the physical touch. Something even more sexy is buying a nice card, pumping her gas, asking her to take a day off, planning a nice day and paying her for her day off. Sexy can also be treating her on days other than her birthday or a holiday. Make a grab bag with little notes in it for her to choose to her liking. These are gifts or things that she likes. I know I'm explaining physical touch, but by doing these, she'll still feel it mentally, which is much more intense than physical touch and then makes the physical part irresistible when the time comes. You have to remember to prepare her mind overall.

- *Receiving gifts* – Don't present just any gift and make sure that you put thought into the gift. Again, time is crucial when delivering. You should know what they like, the worst thing you can do with reference to gifts is to buy something that they already have plenty of. Don't be cheap, I'm not saying be very expensive either, but being cheap shows your lack of concern or your trait of being selfish and struggling to be a giver. Sometimes leaving a gift when they are not expecting it is just as important as giving one in person. Women love surprises. You can also place them strategically around the house or in her car, or if you're trusted enough, leave a gift at her job.

In summary of Seasons and Reasons, I convey to you that prior to implementing and becoming aware of any desired expectations, you must first become intimately familiar with your partner's childhood and history. Your precise communication and kind delivery are crucial during this timeframe. In knowing and understanding their childhood, you can now perceive and comprehend the indicators of their foundation and moral compass, or lack thereof. If you feel that you do not want to or do not have the time to discuss this with your partner or future companion, then they'll never arrive in your season equipped with the proper tools that you deem necessary for a healthy relationship. If they do arrive unprepared, then you're destined to encounter relationship mismatch. The reason for your quest for knowledge about their childhood is essential to developing an affectionate, devoted, and adoring connection with them – a *real* and *genuine* connection. People enter into the lives of others with many issues at times, and in some cases, they come to you and have not gotten over their past or received any form of counseling with respect to relationships, but more importantly, regarding their inability to relate to many things, on both sides. And if they haven't received any counseling or refuse to be open and honest with you, you need to know that this means that they are still harboring that brokenness from childhood and may still refuse counseling later in life as an adult and your partner. While they remain and live in their past, without any deference to you to get help they need, they will continue to project their own intergenerational traits of not only their family violence, but also inherited shadow traits – their *dark side* – onto you. Earlier in my book, I spoke about shadow behavior, these are traits. Their shadow traits include, but are not limited to:

- Lust
- Envy
- Greed
- Deception
- Addictions
- Abusiveness
- Anger
- Possible serial cheating
- Pathological lying
- Violence
- Micro-aggression
- Indecisiveness
- A lack of clarity
- A lack of communication
- Secrecy

Always remember to be careful and mindful in *how giving* you are in your season, because there are people that will be attracted to your financial season and that becomes their "reason"!

Hear My Soul Through My Words

Baby, listening to you, I am no longer confused.

I see you and I want you to see me.

That's not all we need to get to eternity.

You see—deep down inside, I yearn for a connection,

your direction, your affection, and it's not about an erection,

but more importantly, a detection, one of protection, and reflection.

I see you in me, and me in you, but saying it is just hard to do.

Please hear me out, as I convey to you,

my hurt, my pain, my wishes, my strain

to be the one for you, and you for me—that's eternity.

I'm an open book, just take a look, deeper and deeper—

keep her to keep her—read my words,

you come first, I come second,

no outside interferences, there are no thirds.

Take heed to my voice, lift me up, help me grow.

Just like two birds, those wonderful dove's

Hear My Soul—Through My Words!

Summary

Welcome aboard. After all that we have spoken about and, hopefully, after you've considered them, there are a few things that I would like to leave you with. The first one is something that I discovered during my soul-searching and quest to be a better person, a better man, father, uncle, godfather, friend, but most importantly, a loving, genuine and honest partner – a man who wants monogamy, exclusivity, and a heart-to-heart, mind-to-mind, and soul-to-soul body of two, equaling ONE!

Our personalities are hardwired to who we are, and even if we try our best to change, we'll revert back to that hardwiring. However, our Shadow Traits can be changed. Learning and changing your Shadow Traits will allow you to implement new ways, ideas, and begin a new life just when you think that there's no way of changing. I did it, so I know you can too.

Either you do it for a better life, a better husband, or a better wife. Just like a muddy bucket (your muddied mind), as you continue to fill it with clear, fresh, new water, the mud spills out of the bucket. It's a continuous pouring into your life and mind. As you pour, your mind will empty out into others, but mainly into your partner, with fresh, soothing passion, commitment, compassion, and a new beginning. Yes, you have to rehearse this daily, wanting to live right, through the hurt and pain of "starting over." It's an exercise and a mindset. Even if it's with a new person, like I mentioned earlier in my book, we can shed old skin, old ways, and old people. Sometimes, we remain with the same dysfunctional, unhappy, angry, sick, evil person who wants you or anyone else to be their crutch, always rendering them assistance and that's who we become.

When you hope, you make your desired outcome the responsibility of others, and in doing so, you let the negative energy of a broken person diminish your hopes and wishes and you relinquish all strength and possibilities of change. They do not possess the requisite skills or desires to better themselves, yet you wait! They have now become your shadow as well. As your shadow is always with you, so is the person you enable. Words have shadows too; envision and select the most powerful and positively meaningful ones that will help you drive your life and relationship forward. You can become a positive shadow alongside great and healthy people, do so!

Knowing when to move on and stop being afraid to cast that old shadow is an art. Control your emotions, and doubts, then think about "what is" and not "what was." Some people could care less about what is and what was; you must pay attention to this and not stay so long that you lose yourself, drive, integrity, and character. Women, more so than men, will hold on to time, potential, and a false vision. Some potential is "IMPOTENT"! Once you see (like I mentioned earlier about relationship vows) the relationship has begun to become depleted of goodwill, respect, care, and love, that's your first clue that either one of you is losing interest. The first thing that goes is honesty, in which one of you has forgotten about, failed to adhere to or honor the "Relationship Vows." You must take constant inventory of and discuss the relationship vows. Once you put them on the shelf, your relationship follows. Just like old clothes, you can also find a great person or partner in "vintage" – in this context, referring to old, recognized, enduring interests, importance, and quality!

Conclusion

In the end, a healthy, happy, and sustained relationship is a product of the nature and efforts of the persons involved. The truth remains that a total absence of vanity makes a person much more worth your while and attractive in a relationship, especially for those who have been told all their life how good they look or how attractive they are. So, when praised, they refuse to succumb to the vile thrills of egotistical self-absorption of those clambering to attach themselves to conceit. These non-vain types are few, yet genuine. Their essence of beauty lies within and will never be a match for people that do not possess the internal fortitude of soul, purpose, honesty, or reality.

Even if our souls were visible on the exterior, the attractions would remain the same. However, there would still remain the absence of realness due to our inability to extract who our spirit really is. The eyes, without a solid foundation or moral compass will fool the mind, every time!

Ladies, there are many ways that you can keep your man/woman or get a partner and keep them. It's not always about the sex or your physical attributes. Once we transition pass the physical part of your being, especially good or great sex, there are other major components that will keep a persons attention—thus allowing us to mature to the level of becoming your equal, in the realm of womanhood—but you must know!

Don't raise your partner's blood pressure or your voice. Allow them to be themselves, regardless of who you think they should be. You are not the creator, yet you are creative on the vehicle of the creator—to think anything else, the connection and chemistry you desire will ultimately be null and void. Your vision for them has nothing to do with what has been passed down. Their inner workings are far more important to growth in a relationship than your wishes, demands, and expectations. Be patient! Shadow traits, the negative ones, will surface; that's where your vision should be focused on and nowhere else!

Consequently, trying to be someone's mother will prove to be counterproductive. You might surely not be a match in relation to their mother, but it may behoove you still to instill in yourself her style of nurturing. They have or had a mother, or just might be upset with her—in any case, be mindful. Your partner might get over their anguish towards mom, then again, they might not. In both cases, look to improve the mindset and the grooming of their mother, but more importantly, all womanly instincts. Without that plan or attempt, you'll never become a partner but a cohabitant!

Be a genuine companion, confidant, builder, buddy, friend, lover, and nothing else. The aforementioned traits will accomplish many things, but most importantly, it will increase our respect for you. Respect, as in, we will not want another person in any aspect! Believe me, there are women out here that listen to our hurt and pain and will act in the opposite manner from you just to see a man/woman smile and be happy...and that's possibly all she wants to do, all the while slowly paying enough into them, that will give them strength to walk away from you. You have the same qualities that she has, it's just that she uses them in favor of the other person more often than not, and not "her" own favor. She's just more understanding. Granted, your partner may have hurt you, cheated, lied, etc., but give them a chance to right their wrongs. Your imperfections can be just as harmful to them. As men, we process pain, hurt, neglect, and lies differently than women do, so it's important to take note of that! Your feelings and emotions run deep, not only in your heart and mind, but also in your soul and spirit. Ours can be very superficial until we undo the teachings of machismo and chauvinism. Some women fill an anger void by punishing their man when in reality, she sees her absent father and the one who abused her mother in her current man.

"All men are dogs" is by far one of the most overstated phrases in the world. The dogs were once puppies! By all accounts, women can and have typically formed an environment in which little boys were raised. All dogs were once puppies, and if spanked enough, they'll turn and bite you.

"All women spank puppies" is an overrated statement and words which have never really been spoken, yet have some truth! We must be fair in all aspects, whether you like it or not. Societal norms can be devastating!

You can't change what your dad did to your mom, all you can do is make yourself better for your man/woman and not always be guarded! Stop thinking that their money is your money unless you discuss that with them, and even still, it's your partners to share, keep, invest, and make!

Don't expect to take anything from them, reducing anyone by a small percentage, in any way, then expect them to be 100%. That which you took—let's say 25% of anything—will reduce their capabilities!

We want to love you as a whole and nothing less. The more you build into us, the stronger, happier, and more giving we become. We fear not being 360! Treat us as your wishes guide you, and not as things or people have conditioned you to react!

TWO BODIES BEING ONE…NOT SOMEBODY—NOT EVERYBODY

YOU MUST EMBODY

WELCOME ABOARD THE LOVESHIP, OUR NEXT STOP… ETERNAL BLISS!